WORLD WAR 2 FOR TEENS

AMAZING FACTS, KEY PLAYERS, HEROIC ACTS, MAJOR BATTLES, AND HOW THE WAR CHANGED THE WORLD

JAMES BURROWS

CONTENTS

Introduction ix

1. WHAT CAUSED WORLD WAR 2? 1
The Treaty of Versailles 2
Economic Crisis 2
Nationalism, Fascism, and Statism 4
The League of Nations 6
Munich Agreement 7

2. WHO WERE THE NAZIS? 9
The German Workers' Party 9
Hitler's Rise to Power 10
Aryan Race 12
The Gestapo and SS 14

3. WHICH COUNTRIES TOOK PART IN THE WAR? 17
Axis Powers 18
Allied Powers 19

4. LEADERS AND GENERALS 23
Allied Political Leaders and Military Generals 24
Axis Political Leaders and Military Generals 31

5. WORLD WAR 2 IN NUMBERS 39
Shocking Numbers 39
Surprising Amounts 40

6. TIMELINE OF THE WAR 43
1939 43
1940 44
1941 46
1942 47
1943 49
1944 50
1945 51

7. MAJOR EVENTS AND BATTLES—1939 53
Invasion of Poland 54
Evacuation of Children in Britain 55
Battle of the Atlantic 56
Winter War 58
Battle of the River Plate 59

8. MAJOR EVENTS AND BATTLES—1940 61
Invasion of Norway 61
The Battle of France 62
Dunkirk 64
The Battle of Britain 65
The Blitz 67

9. MAJOR EVENTS AND BATTLES—1941 71
Operation Barbarossa 71
Siege of Leningrad 73
Attack on Pearl Harbor 75

10. MAJOR EVENTS AND BATTLES—1942 79
Internment Starts in America 79
Bombing of Cologne 80
Battle of Midway 81
Battle of Stalingrad 83
Battle of Guadalcanal 85
Battle of El Alamein 87
Operation Torch 89

11. MAJOR EVENTS AND BATTLES—1943 91
Warsaw Ghetto Uprising 91
Battle of Kursk 93
Operation Husky 94
Italian Campaign 95

12. MAJOR EVENTS AND BATTLES—1944 97
Battle of Monte Cassino 97
Operation Argument—"Big Week" 99
Operation Overlord—"D-Day" 100
Operation Bagration 104
Operation Market Garden 106
Battle of the Bulge 107

13. HOW THE WAR ENDED 111
Battle of Iwo Jima 111
Battle of Okinawa 112
Fall of Berlin 114
The Atomic Bombings 117

14. HEROIC FEATS 121
Military 121
Spies and Resistance Fighters 126
Humanitarians 128
Scientists 129

15. PRISONERS OF WAR 131
The Third Geneva Convention, 1929 131
Germany 132
Japan 133
Russia 134
America 135
Britain 136
Famous POW's Prison Escapes 137

16. THE HOLOCAUST 139
Why Did the Nazis Persecute the Jews? 139
Kristallnacht 140
Ghettos 141
Concentration Camps 142
Anne Frank 144
The End and Aftermath 145

17. HOW THE WAR CHANGED THE WORLD 147
Geo-Political 147
Society 149
Technology 150
United Nations and WHO 151
The Cold War 151

Conclusion 153
References 155
About the Author 169

Dedicated to my grandfather, George,
who spent four years as a German prisoner of war,
after capture at Tobruk.

INTRODUCTION

The Second World War shook the entire earth.

Spanning the globe, its effects were seen in so many ways. Lasting six years, it was the most devastating and costly war that has ever been fought. Claiming up to 70 million lives, more than double the number of those lost in WWI, it left a mark that was felt for many generations to come.

Fought between the Axis powers of imperialist and fascist countries (Germany, Japan, and Italy) and the uneasy combination of Allies (Britain, the United States, and the Soviet Union, along with others), the war spread over much of the world map to include virtually every country. It pitted old rivals against each other while creating alliances between enemies.

Old European powers that had reigned over the political stage for so long, were brought to their knees, while new superpowers like the United States and the Soviet Union rose to take charge. This shift of ideologies would later result in a new conflict called the Cold War where democracy and communism took center stage.

The advances in science, warfare, and industry not only revolutionized the way soldiers fought and wars were conducted, but also saw the advent of modern genocide where millions of people were tortured, gassed, and killed in Nazi concentration camps. It was also the birth of military technologies that would ultimately wipe out entire cities in the form of atomic bombs. Instead of being contained to soldier on soldier, WW2 stretched across the normal lines of military engagement as civilians were thrown into the deadly mix resulting in more non-combatant deaths than ever before.

Starting with Germany's invasion of Poland in 1939, Hitler made it clear that he was intent on expanding his influence across Europe. By 1941, this had become a reality as the Nazis racked up several decisive victories. Japan forced the United States to enter the war in 1942 after they led surprise attacks against them to conquer most of the Pacific region. It looked as though the Axis powers would dominate the world.

But things began to turn as Germany decided to push deep into the Soviet Union, finding themselves fighting on too many fronts. Japan felt the sting as the United States mobilized and began taking back key areas. Slowly, the Axis powers were forced to give up their trophies and retreat into their own countries. By 1945, the writing was on the wall—Italy had already surrendered, Germany was completely overrun, and Japan suffered the heavy blow of two of its cities being devastated by atomic bombs.

This book will give you more than just the dates, facts, and figures, it will fill in the exciting stories of what happened, by revealing the gritty details of how the battles were won, and paint vivid pictures of the key players. After reading this, you will know about:

- The causes of the war and who was involved.
- The major battles and the turning points of the war, along with statistics and incredible stories of heroism.
- The rise and fall of Adolf Hitler; his ambitions, mistakes, and twisted ideologies that saw him win stunning victories as well as perpetrate some of the worst atrocities ever seen.
- Winston Churchill's inspiring stand against the Germans as he rallied Britain to fight against the evil of the Axis powers.
- America's reluctance to join the conflict and how the Japanese bombing of Pearl Harbor forced their hand, which would end up shifting the direction of the war.
- The Soviet Union's part in WW2 and their Red Army as they held off the Nazis in the Siege of Leningrad during the bitter Russian winter.
- The Holocaust and how Hitler tried to wipe out the Jews in a systematic strategy of death.

Filled with incredible stories, you will find yourself back in the middle of the Second World War; face to face with leaders who shaped the course of history, fighting alongside soldiers in the heat of battle, and living through extraordinary moments with those who endured.

Also, look out for these add-ons throughout the book with some incredible extra insights into the war:

AMAZING FACTS

Strap on your helmet, tighten your boots, and find out all you can about the moment in history that changed the entire world!

1

WHAT CAUSED WORLD WAR 2?

World War I was supposed to be the "war to end all wars" (Kinder, 2014). But instead of preventing more bloodshed and destruction, it was like a stone being dropped into a pond—the ripples soon became waves of bitterness and discouragement that reached every shore until those countries were once again fighting each other.

Although the date when Hitler invaded Poland and brought Britain and France to declare war against Germany is recorded as the start of WW2, it began soon after the end of the Great War as nations punished Germany and sought ways to avoid another conflict.

The mistrust that was already simmering between certain countries was only increased by many significant actions. These, and other external circumstances, became a boiling pot of ambition and suspicion that would all ultimately lead to another world war.

THE TREATY OF VERSAILLES

The end of WWI was signified by the signing of a treaty that put the blame on those who were responsible for causing it and made sure that they could not start another one. Signed on June 28, 1919, in the Palace of Versailles, Britain, France, Italy, and America (known as the "Big Four") took it upon themselves to hand out the punishments and set the standards (Arun, 2020). But instead of calming the waters, it stirred up anger and dissatisfaction among countries that were criticized or left out of the agreements.

Germany was left to carry most of the blame with harsh conditions imposed, losing almost 15% of its territory, and a reduced army as well as having to repay a massive financial penalty (Arun, 2020). Its people felt humiliated and blamed the treaty for the suffering it faced as a result.

Japan and Italy also found themselves out in the cold as they were not involved in the negotiations and their concerns were not acknowledged. Instead of being given land that had been promised for its assistance in WWI, Italy was overlooked and felt as though its dreams of being a great nation once again, had been ignored (Arun, 2020).

Japan too, had helped in the war and expected their contributions to be honored, but it was left empty handed. This caused it to become bitter against those countries that had made all the decisions.

ECONOMIC CRISIS

The effects of a worldwide economic depression were felt across the globe as countries struggled with rising costs and inflation after WWI. There was little in the way of real commodities, and for over a year, nations struggled to overcome this deficit. Many soldiers took time to adjust back to normal civilian life, affecting the workforce.

As part of the treaty's conditions, Germany had to repay a massive penalty of $31 billion (Arun, 2020). Not only was this an extremely large sum of money, but their infrastructure and industry were still trying to recover from the damage the country had suffered because of the war. The economic hardships that followed caused the country to sink into a financial depression with very high unemployment.

AMAZING FACTS

- *The price of food doubled almost every four days. A loaf of bread that cost 163 marks in 1922 ended up costing 200 billion a year later (Smith, 2016)! This hyperinflation pushed many people onto the streets and was a breeding ground for bitterness and dissatisfaction toward the West.*
- *The value of money dropped so quickly that people had to be paid twice a day.*

Because of the economic problems felt in many countries, fascist groups grew stronger. People wanted to take action, take back what they felt was theirs, and see economic growth. Fascism promised this, and so, support for similar factions in Hungary, Romania, and other European countries grew.

Later, the Great Depression of 1930 hit America after the stock market crashed. This sent a shockwave throughout the world economy and had a devastating effect on every country. People began to blame governments for their troubles and looked for answers from anyone that could give them. This desperation caused by poverty, unemployment, and hunger led many to follow groups that promised stability and victory.

NATIONALISM, FASCISM, AND STATISM

There was a growing dislike for western democracy and the way it had crippled the smaller countries. It opened gaping holes in communities where people began to group together and talk about restoring the pride of their nation and bringing it back to its glory days. Liberal policies such as freedom of choice, liberty, and democracy were exchanged for more extreme right-wing ideals of force, anti-capitalism, and state rule.

- The idea of *nationalism* revolves around a country becoming fiercely patriotic to the point of ignoring other countries and believing it is, in some way, better than others. The state becomes everything, with devoted loyalty to its cause above any group or person.
- *Fascism* comes from a Latin word that means a bundle of sticks tied together around an ax, meaning people should give up their individual rights for the good of the state. Usually, it revolves around a perception that a certain religion or race is better than the rest. A dictator often controls the government, and there's no tolerance of disagreement.
- The notion of *statism* is basically a mix of these two ideals where the state controls all the industrial, economic, and social affairs of the country. Often, it involves a puppet government, allowing those who are in control to make decisions behind the scenes.

Italy

All within the state, nothing outside the state, nothing against the state.
–Benito Mussolini

When Benito Mussolini helped to form a political group during WWI, it was to encourage nationalism and bring his country back to its days as the Roman Empire. Having been pushed aside during the Paris Peace Treaty, and facing the growth of communist beliefs, Italians began to look for something more conservative. The Fascist Party grew in number and strength, and in 1922, seized power in their "March to Rome" where Mussolini declared himself the Prime Minister (Arun, 2020).

Three years later, he had ousted the king and set himself up as dictator. He found allies in Germany and Japan as they too began to seek similar aims for their countries.

Germany

Only childish and naïve minds can lull themselves in the idea that they can bring about a correction of Versailles by wheedling and begging… No nation can remove this hand from its throat except by the sword. –Adolf Hitler

Weakened after WWI, the people could not trust democracy or their own monarchy, and so, turned to promises of a stronger nation in groups like the Nationalist Socialist Workers' Party, or "Nazi Party" as they were called (Arun, 2020). Adolf Hitler was a charismatic leader, and his ideas of racial purity began to take hold in people's minds. Believing in their superiority as a German people, the citizens began to follow this ultra-patriotic and fascist movement.

In 1932, Hitler's party had become the largest in the German government, and within a year, he was made the Reich Chancellor, the leader of the country. The Nazis had taken over through national pride and militaristic methods.

Japan

Almost 60 years before the end of WWI, the political idea of statism had been brewing in Japan. It was a mix of nationalistic pride, militarizing the people, and belief in restoring past glory by expanding their territories. When the Treaty of Versailles was signed and international naval agreements were made, Japan was not acknowledged as an equal among the Western powers, and this was the turning point that led to a renewed interest in statism (Arun, 2020). It wanted a specific mention of racial equality to be included in the policies that were being drawn up to ensure that Japanese immigrants in America were treated fairly, but this was rejected.

The result in Japan was that anyone who showed democratic tendencies was assassinated or arrested. Liberal ideals were pushed aside, and anyone following these liberal practices was targeted. A few attempts were made to overthrow the government, and in the end, the Emperor became more of a figurehead than an actual ruler. An all-out attack on China as part of its expansion plans followed.

THE LEAGUE OF NATIONS

President Woodrow Wilson's idea of countries banding together to avoid further war was an admirable one, but it lacked any real power to act. Established as an organization of nations to preserve peace in the world, it brought all the major players together to decide on international events. Britain and France agreed, in principle, to the idea but would not put themselves at the mercy of other countries, meaning no one could challenge them. This made the

League of Nations weak, and some even called it the "League of Victors" instead (Arun, 2020).

The biggest failure of this organization came when it failed to stop the expansion of the three countries that would ultimately become the Axis powers. Japan invaded Manchuria in 1931, Italy attacked Ethiopia in 1935, and Germany ignored the treaty's conditions by occupying the Rhineland in 1936, and annexing Austria in 1938. On all three accounts, the League of Nations did nothing to stop these countries from expanding their territories. Rather than maintaining peace, it made these nations feel that they could continue down this path of expanding territories.

MUNICH AGREEMENT

As a way to try and avoid war, leaders like Britain's Neville Chamberlain went as far as appeasing Hitler's demand for more land. Rather than seeing conflict, an agreement was signed giving Germany full ownership of the Sudetenland, a German-speaking region within the borders of Czechoslovakia.

In September 1938, Britain, France, Italy, and Germany signed the pact without inviting the Soviet Union or Czechoslovakia to be a part of it (Parkin, 2018). It surprised Hitler that his demands were met so easily, and he pushed this weak foreign policy as far as he could to get as much of the land he wanted without having to fight for it. Later, Hitler would ignore any promises not to invade the rest of Czechoslovakia, and he swallowed up the rest of the country into his expanding empire. Instead of the peace that Chamberlain celebrated after signing the Munich Agreement, it showed the failure of appeasement and the League of Nations to act when necessary.

With all these conditions in place, the world was set on a course that headed straight toward another world war.

2

WHO WERE THE NAZIS?

With all the discontent and discouragement in Germany after WWI, the people looked for someone who could promise them a way out of their troubles, who could assure them that they would once again be a proud nation, who could lead them to be a victorious nation once again—that person was Adolf Hitler.

By using the circumstances that surrounded him at the time, the dire state of the economy, and dissatisfaction with the government, a strategy of fear through highly motivated guards, and some back-handed tactics, Hitler maneuvered a small group of workers called the Nazis into the strongest ruling party of the day. Today, the swastika, the iron cross, and the uniform all signify a highly determined and disciplined, but racist and cold-blooded force.

THE GERMAN WORKERS' PARTY

After the humiliating defeat of the First World War, there was little respect left for the old, aging ideas of an emperor and king as they had had under Kaiser Wilhelm II. The people wanted change.

Anton Drexler, a locksmith, saw the need to unite the workers as a group to have their voices heard, and in 1919, the German Workers' Party began (Encyclopedia Britannica, 2018a). Hitler attended one of its meetings and saw a chance for him to align his ideas with a movement already in place.

Because he had been a soldier in the war, as well as his charismatic way of speaking, the party members respected and listened to his ideologies. Within a year, he had taken over the party, renaming it the Nationalist Socialist German Workers' Party and laying down 25 economic points and a foreign policy that would become their manifesto (Encyclopedia Britannica, 2018a).

The group adopted a very clear anti-Semitic (anti-Jewish) stance which Hitler would use to blame all the wrongs of society on. In short, the Nazis believed that they were doing the world a favor by getting rid of communism, democracy, capitalism, and the Jewish people (Encyclopedia Britannica, 2019). The rallies that were held drew many people, and in 1923, Hitler thought he had enough support to overthrow the ruling powers. The party staged what was called the Beer Hall Revolt, but it was an unsuccessful attempt to take over the Bavarian government, and the military was called in to restore order (Encyclopedia Britannica, 2018a). The result was that Hitler was jailed and his party disbanded.

HITLER'S RISE TO POWER

Instead of a setback, Hitler used his time in prison to write down his ideas and publish a book called *Mein Kampf* (My Struggle) (National WW2 Museum, 2022a). After he was released, he decided to rebuild the Nazis as a political group that would gain power through the correct channels. This reorganization changed it from a group of angry protestors to a legitimate party, and its fame and numbers grew dramatically from 25,000 to 180,000 members over the next four years (Encyclopedia Britannica, 2018a). But even though their numbers increased, they did not perform very well at the elections until the worldwide economic crisis hit.

The Great Depression was the Nazis' first big steppingstone into power as unemployment soared. People were desperate for answers and liked what they heard in Hitler's speeches about nationalism and rebuilding the country. He was a brilliant, dynamic speaker and could hold his audience for long periods. Many people were swayed by his words and his charisma as a leader. With increased campaigning, the party increased its votes in the Reichstag (German Parliament) elections to a massive 14,000,000, making them the largest by far (Encyclopedia Britannica, 2018a).

However, not all the tactics Hitler used were above board, and a number of behind-the-scenes acts were used to push his group to the front.

- Convincing the president to name him chancellor, gave Hitler the power to consolidate the Nazis into government.
- The Reichstag building suspiciously caught fire and burned down only a few days before the 1933 elections, which Hitler blamed on the communists. He used this to convince the president to issue a state of emergency suspending freedom of the press and other liberties (National WW2 Museum, 2022a).
- The military arm of the Nazis, the SA (stormtroopers), used force and terror against anyone opposing them. Many were afraid to vote against them and did not turn out to vote at all.
- Without a clear majority, Hitler passed the Enabling Act which allowed him to issue laws without the government's consent. This gave his party full authority without needing to ask for it.

Soon after, the Nazis were declared to be the only political party, making it a one-party state, and soon Hitler became the Führer (Leader) after the president's death in 1934 (National WW2 Museum, 2022a). Germany had effectively become a totalitarian state with Hitler as its dictator.

ARYAN RACE

Hitler never shifted from his beliefs right up until the end, he stuck to the points that he laid out and expected all of Germany to follow without question. One of the most prominent ideas that he preached was the notion that pure Germans were born of an Aryan race. Any other race was considered to be "subhuman" in Hitler's eyes—this included Jews and the Slavic people of Russia as well as homosexuals and those with handicaps (National WW2 Museum, 2022a).

Pure-blooded Aryans were believed to be those who had descended from ancient Nordic people with specific qualities. Blue eyes, blonde hair, and well-built human beings were what the Nazis aspired to be, which is ironic considering Hitler had none of these features!

In his attempt to produce a pure nation, Hitler sent out expeditions to Tibet and allowed scientists to conduct experiments on subjects to find out the origins and genes of these supposedly racially superior people (BBC, 2021). It was so important to him because his entire philosophy of blaming the Jews and exalting the Germans rested upon this idea. He believed that they were called to rule for 1,000 years in a new order called the Third Reich.

A large part of preparing the German nation for this ideal was to get rid of anyone who was not purebred. This resulted in large-scale ethnic cleansing, and ultimately led to "the Final Solution," a plan that would exterminate the Jews and any other undesirables from the country.

It was this idea of a pure bloodline descending from the Aryan race that caused Hitler to adopt the swastika. Although the emblem has come to represent the racist and fascist beliefs of the Nazis, its origins were not so stark and cold-blooded.

Instead of bloodshed and hatred, it was originally used to send the message of positivity. The ancient Sanskrit meaning of the word "svastika" means to encourage well-being and not the superiority of a race as Hitler wanted it to be used (Hogeback, 2019). From its earliest roots, the swastika, a four-legged cross with the arms bent at 90 degrees, conveyed fertility and life, which is in total contrast to the death that's associated with Nazi Germany in WW2. But after the truth of the Schutzstaffel and their work in the concentration camps became known, it has become synonymous with death and anti-Semitism.

AMAZING FACTS

- *Years before Hitler adopted the logo, it could be seen in Hindu and Buddhist temples, Coca-Cola adverts, Girl Scout magazines, and even U.S. military troops and R.A.F. planes (Campion, 2014).*

THE GESTAPO AND SS

Despite Hitler's attempts to legally gain power as a political party, he needed extra help to convince people to support his ideals. The only way to do this was through fear and force, something that's often found in fascist governments. Although the Nazis already had a strong-arm group called the SA (brown shirts or stormtroopers) to coerce people, Hitler realized that they would need extra units that could go deeper and further than these could.

The Schutzstaffel or "Protective Echelon" (SS) was a uniformed and elite corps that dressed in black, were given incredible power to carry out their tasks, and had three main divisions: The Allgemeine-SS looked after general policing, the Waffen-SS was a specialized combat unit in the military, and the Death Squad oversaw the running of the concentration camps. The Gestapo was a smaller sub-division of this large-scale policing unit.

Hermann Göring, one of Hitler's right-hand men, had reorganized army units to form one special branch of political police under his personal command, which he called the Gestapo (Encyclopedia Britannica, 2018b). Their main objective was to infiltrate and weed out any opposition and send anyone that was a Jew or acted against the party to the camps.

Heinrich Himmler was given command of the SS, and in 1936, reshuffled the police forces into one maze of security branches including the Gestapo (Encyclopedia Britannica, 2018b). Within this overlapping hierarchy, the Gestapo often got away with any actions they committed and were not held accountable to any office for their harsh treatment of anyone they suspected may be committing treason. Mostly, they relied on people in the community for information alerting them to anti-Nazi behavior from their own neighbors. The punishment was either a swift death or a long journey to the concentration camps.

The SS as a whole was so committed and single-minded in carrying out their duties, that even when the war had ended, many of the officers still believed that they had done nothing wrong. Col. Joachim Peiper, one of the most feared Waffen-SS commanders who ordered and committed mass murders of any prisoners he caught during the war like the Malmedy Massacre, remained loyal to the cause years after the war saying, *"I was a National-Socialist [Nazi] and I remain one"* (Admin, 2021).

3

WHICH COUNTRIES TOOK PART IN THE WAR?

Countries from across the globe took part in WW2. Some of them charged in, ready to fight for their cause; others joined reluctantly halfway through, and still more were forced into fighting because they were simply caught in the middle of it all. A few remained neutral, choosing not to get involved. But the wide-spread mix of soldiers that came from every corner of the world made this the largest war by far.

As in any war, there were two main sides: the Axis Powers who had started by attacking their neighbors and conquering land for themselves, and the Allied Powers who responded to the threats and invasions to stop them from going any further. In each side there were the main players, with many others that joined willingly or were roped in because of some vested interests they had.

In total, around 157 million soldiers were called up to serve in the military for their respective sides.

AXIS POWERS

This is often known as the evil side because they were the first to break the terms of the Treaty of Versailles, invaded other countries, disregarded any chance of peace, and in the end, lost! Not only that, but the main players of Germany, Italy, and Japan were all dictatorships in some way or another. Five other European countries joined in to assist these three in their quest for glory.

Three Main Players

Germany was by far the largest contingent of this group with almost 18 million fighting for the Third Reich. In defiance of the Treaty of Versailles, Hitler started mobilizing his troops and adding numbers to his army. The peace accord did not allow Germany to unite its forces with Austria, stripping Germany down to only 100,000 men, 15,000 in the navy, a total restriction on any air force, and very little in the way of heavy military equipment (Arun, 2020). Basically, the country was denied any chance to fight!

Not only that, but he had already marched into Austria, and claimed it as part of his greater Germany. Although this was forbidden by the treaty, no one did anything to stop him.

Italy also felt some of the harsh limitations of the treaty and was forbidden from invading Abyssinia (Ethiopia). In 1936, Germany allied itself with Italy as they both had similar goals, and Mussolini and Hitler formed the Rome-Berlin Axis, setting themselves against those countries who supported the peace agreement (USHMM, 2022). As part of their contribution, Italy brought about 9 million soldiers to the war effort.

Japan's aim was to become an empire to be reckoned with, sharing the same ideals as Germany, they became allies in what was called the Anti-Comintern Pact (USHMM, 2022). Italy also joined this agreement a year later, but it was only in September

1940 that the three countries formally united as a military force under the Tripartite Pact, and became known as the Axis Powers (USHMM, 2022). As a country, Japan brought another 9 million fighting men to the table.

Five Other Countries

At this point, the Soviet Union was friendly with Germany, having secured their own agreement to not attack each other, even though Japan had issues with the Russians. All of that changed when Hitler decided to ignore this pact and march toward Moscow. To pull off this daring invasion, Germany would need more support and soldiers, and ended up making promises and putting lots of pressure on Hungary, Croatia, Bulgaria, Slovakia, and Romania to join the Axis Powers (USHMM, 2022).

Hungary had been given part of Czechoslovakia, and so, had little choice but to align itself with Germany and Italy. Romania supported the idea of invading the Soviets as this would eliminate the communist threat, so they also jumped into the coalition along with Slovakia which depended very heavily on Germany to remain a separate country.

Bulgaria was not quick to enter the alliance and had to be promised Greek territory to join the group. Croatia was run by fascists after Yugoslavia was invaded and split up, and they willingly combined its forces with Germany's. Finland assisted Germany in its bid to regain territory that the Soviets had captured a few years before.

ALLIED POWERS

Although these countries ultimately won the war, they were not necessarily always the strongest. At times, they were outnumbered and suffered heavy defeats in certain battles, but once they all functioned together on the same side, they proved too much for the Axis Powers to hold back. Not only that, but they generally (apart from the communist Soviets) were all in favor of democracy.

Four Key Countries

Britain and France were the first to stand up to Germany, and so formed the base of this alliance. Once the Soviet Union and the United States joined in the fight, the Allies' combined military strength was far greater than that of its enemy, and this shift in manpower and weaponry could clearly be seen from 1942 onward. Many other countries such as Australia, South Africa, and India all contributed to the war effort as well.

Britain's attempts to appease Hitler had obviously failed as it was clear that he was not going to stop. After Germany had entered Austria, taken back the Rhineland, and forced Czechoslovakia to give up large parts of its country, an assurance was given to Poland that any threat to its borders would be counted as an act of aggression and be answered in kind. When Germany invaded the country in 1939, Britain and France immediately declared war, setting themselves up against the Axis Powers. Britain committed a force of 6 million men to fight against the Nazis while France could only muster just over 3 million.

Josef Stalin, the Soviet leader, had signed a nonaggression pact in August 1939 which meant that they would assist Hitler in the invasion of Poland, and in return, be given part of the conquered country (History, 2009). This caused concern among the Allies as they had to consider whether the Russians would be an enemy with a massive force of 21 million soldiers. But Stalin was content in the meantime in securing Poland and focusing on conquering Finland.

It was only in June 1941, that Operation Barbarossa swung the Soviets onto the Allied side of the war (History, 2009). Hitler's invasion of Russia made his intentions clear, and the nonaggression pact was dissolved. With the Soviet's Red Army fully behind Britain and France's attempts to stop the German expansion, Hitler faced a war on two fronts.

Up to this point, the United States was reluctant to join the battle that raged in Europe because it was busy focusing on its own internal politics. With its superior navy and air force, it could match the might of the Japanese army that had begun invading more of China and smaller Pacific islands. However, it was not until the surprise attack on Pearl Harbor on December 7, 1941, by Japanese aircraft, that America finally declared war on the Axis Powers (History.com, 2009). They brought an extra 16 million soldiers to the fight!

Others Involved

There were 14 countries that chose to remain neutral during the war including Sweden, Portugal, and Switzerland. However, more than 40 pledged allegiances to stop the German Nazis, Italian Fascists, and Japanese Imperialists and gave their support in some way or another. Here are a few stories of their contributions:

- As part of the British Empire, India's role in helping the war effort is one that has been overlooked. The Gurkhas and Sikhs were renowned as fearless fighters, and they were part of over 2 million soldiers that volunteered to go to war (Simha, 2016). Not only did they provide significant manpower, but they were also one of the largest contributors of raw materials to keep the war effort alive.

Field Marshal Claude Auchinleck said that Britain *"couldn't have come through both wars if they hadn't had the Indian Army"* (Simha, 2016).

• One million Australian men and women served in the war, with at least half of those being actively involved (RSL NSW, 2019). The navy, air force, and army all faced combat in different regions from Italy to the Battle of Britain, and throughout the Mediterranean and North Africa. As a country, it faced attacks from Japanese planes and submarines on Northern Australia and Sydney Harbor.

But its most well-known stand-off against the Germans was in the Libyan Port of Tobruk where 14,000 Australians survived repeated attacks from the enemy, gaining them the nickname, "Rats of Tobruk" (RSL NSW, 2019).

• As a former colony of Britain, South Africa entered the war and fought in many different locations and divisions much as Australia did. In North Africa, it suffered many defeats but finally held out against fierce German fighting under the brilliant desert strategist, Field Marshal Erwin Rommel. Its contribution was seen as a "*sacrifice [that] resulted in the turning point of the battle, giving the Allies the upper hand in North Africa at that time*" (Beyer, 2022b).

U.S. General Mark W. Clark said that the South African 6th Armored Division was a "*battle-wise outfit, bold and aggressive against the enemy… despite their comparatively small numbers, they never complained about losses*" (Beyer, 2022b).

AMAZING FACTS

- *Marmaduke "Pat" Prattle, a South African, is recorded as being the top ace as an RAF pilot, even though he was shot down and killed in 1941. He had a personal total of 41 kills, but many claim that the number is closer to 60 (Beyer, 2022b)!*

4

LEADERS AND GENERALS

Wars are not just armies, tanks, and planes bombing cities, and taking fire at their enemies. In every vehicle and behind each gun, is a person—wars are fought by individuals. Even though the soldiers face off against their opponents, the real wins and losses are made by those who make the decisions—the generals who strategize and decide when armies should push forward and when they need to pull back!

And even further up the chain, there were leaders, like Hitler and Churchill, whose words and actions mobilized the citizens, military, and entire countries to jump into action.

ALLIED POLITICAL LEADERS AND MILITARY GENERALS

Great Britain

Winston Churchill

Neville Chamberlain's appeasement policy had not worked, instead, it gave Germany and Italy free reign to do exactly what they wanted to do—expand their territories and take over countries without any punishment. Churchill had warned against the Nazi's rise to power, and in 1940 was elected as prime minister when it became clear that action had to be taken.

Winston Churchill

Known as the "British Lion," Churchill was the perfect statesman during the war years (Noy, 2019). Coming into office at a very difficult time when France had just been conquered, Britain faced defeat, and the German U-boat submarines had the Allied ships in trouble, Winston Churchill used his brilliance as a speechmaker to motivate the country to rise and stand up against the attacks.

Two of his most well-known speeches include the following words:

"I would say to the House as I said to those who have joined this government: I have nothing to offer but blood, toil, tears, and sweat." From his first speech as Prime Minister; Westminster, May 13, 1940.

"Never in the field of human conflict was so much owed by so many to so few." From a speech given after the Battle of Britain, recognizing the enormous effort and sacrifice of the pilots and bomber crew in establishing air superiority over England; Westminster, August 20, 1940.

AMAZING FACTS

- *In his younger days, Churchill was a reporter in South Africa during the Boer War. The train he was on was ambushed; he was captured and sent to Pretoria prison. With no map or idea of the country, Churchill slipped past the guards, climbed the fence, and escaped. A large manhunt followed as he hid in coal mines and the bushes until he was smuggled out of South Africa and became a war hero (Klein, 2016).*

Field Marshal Bernard "Monty" Montgomery

Montgomery served in WWI where he was seriously wounded but survived. When the Second World War came, he had risen in rank and was then leading the Eighth Army which fought in North Africa against Rommel. He was always present, visiting the units, chatting with the men, and encouraging them. Soon after that, he was given total command of planning and running the D-Day invasion of Normandy.

United States

Franklin D. Roosevelt

As president, he wanted to assist in the war, but Congress resisted, choosing to remain neutral. Roosevelt initially supplied weapons to Britain and France, and military aid to Russia when

Germany attacked. It was only when Pearl Harbor was attacked that America shifted gears and put all its focus into all-out war production. He died before the end of the war.

President Roosevelt

George Marshall

One of the only military men to be involved in both World Wars as well as the early days of the Cold War. A brilliant strategist, Roosevelt credited him by saying, *"He is the true organizer of victory."* Apart from devising the Meuse-Argonne offensive in WWI and other operations, his most well-known contribution was the Marshall Plan, long-term economic assistance to Europe after the war, which won him a Nobel Peace Prize in 1953 (WGBH, 2019).

General Dwight D. Eisenhower

A five-star general, Eisenhower was responsible for planning and running Operation Torch in North Africa as well as the invasion of France and Germany toward the end of WW2. He became Supreme Allied Commander in Europe in 1943, and despite not always agreeing with Roosevelt and Churchill on political maneuvers, he was successful in all the operations he oversaw (D-Day, n.d.).

Nicknamed "Ike," he never saw action himself but was still highly respected by his men as they recognized his leadership and clever strategic mind. Eisenhower later became President of the United States in 1953 (D-Day, n.d.).

General Douglas MacArthur

Involved in WWI, MacArthur led raids on enemy trenches and gained a reputation as a courageous leader, was promoted to Brigadier General, and led the victorious Meuse-Argonne offensive. A highly decorated officer, he became commander of the U.S. Armed Forces on the Far East and formed a new strategy of island "hopping," where he attacked the Japanese at their weakest spots and not their strongholds which turned out to be very successful (Orlikoff, n.d.).

An outspoken, flamboyant officer, he was never scared to engage in combat and push his men hard to achieve victory. He would later go on to lead the NATO forces in the Korean War.

General George S. Patton

Patton was very involved in WWI and fought on the frontlines with the British Tank Corps where he was shot by a machine gun and received a Purple Heart for his contributions. During the early years of WW2, he convinced Congress that the United States needed to build up its own armed forces, and he was promoted to Major General, in charge of the armored brigade (D-Day, n.d.).

Although he was a harsh commander, his methods produced results, and he won decisive victories against Rommel in Africa. Later in Europe, his actions almost cost him his rank after seemingly encouraging the killing of prisoners and beating up a soldier he thought was a coward. But he continued to be an effective leader as he used the Blitzkrieg method against the Germans during the Normandy invasion. Patton made critical moves in the Battle of the Bulge to relieve troops that were surrounded and put more pressure on the Germans to withdraw back behind their own borders (D-Day, n.d.).

Allied Generals Front: Patton 2nd left, Eisenhower middle

Soviet Union

Josef Stalin

After Lenin died, Stalin took over as part of collective leadership. His Five-Year Plan was meant to centralize the economy and agriculture; however, it had huge effects that led to famine and hunger throughout Russia. From 1934, Stalin ordered the deaths of almost 700,000 people he suspected were enemies in what was called the "Great Purge," which gave him complete control over the entire country and state (D-Day, n.d.).

Josef Stalin

Despite signing a nonaggression pact with Hitler, the German invasion of the Soviet Union resulted in Stalin ordering his Red Army to counterattack and hold off the Nazis. It was the cold winter of Russia, and the size of its army finally pushed Hitler's men back until they had retreated all the way into Germany.

AMAZING FACTS

- *Stalin had a summer retreat built especially for him in Sochi where he could take hydrogen sulfide baths every year to help with musculoskeletal problems he suffered from (D-Day, n.d.).*

General Georgy Zhukov

Zhukov oversaw the defense of Leningrad, Moscow, and Stalingrad as the Germans pushed further into the Soviet Union. He was involved in many of the battles, especially the Battle of Berlin which saw the defeat of the Nazis and brought them to surrender to his forces (D-Day, n.d.).

He called on his soldiers to *"remember our brothers and sisters, our mothers and fathers, our wives and children tortured to death by the Germans. We shall exact a brutal revenge for everything"* (D-Day, n.d.). This resulted in the widespread looting, rape, and murder of German civilians as the Red Army pushed them back into their own country.

General Vasily Chuikov

Chuikov was in command of the Soviet 62nd Army that was involved in the Battle of Stalingrad and because of his achievements there he was promoted to oversee the 8th Guards Army until the end of the war. His unit took heavy casualties as they pushed on toward Berlin where General Krebs arrived with a white flag and told Chuikov that Hitler was dead (LRE, 2022).

He was promoted to Marshal of the Soviet Union and went on to play important roles in the Cuban Missile Crisis of 1962 (LRE, 2022).

France

Charles de Gaulle

A tank division commander during the beginning of the war, de Gaulle warned about certain weaknesses he saw in the French defenses. However, these were not considered, and the German Blitzkrieg broke through forcing France to surrender. De Gaulle's unit was the only one that had any success against the Nazis. He fled to Britain where he assisted in the underground resistance until he became president once France had been freed from the Germans (Noy, 2019).

China

Chiang Kai-Shek

As an anti-communist leader, he was opposed to the uprising during China's civil war, but Kai-Shek put aside his differences to work with his rival once Japan invaded China's mainland in 1937 (Noy, 2019). Halfway through, he ended up fighting Mao, his opponent, as well as the Japanese, and was criticized for his way of fighting by the United States. After the war, he resumed his bitter feud with the communists, but ended up fleeing to Taiwan where he became president.

Mao Zedong

As ruler of the communists in China, Mao was fiercely against Kai-Shek's government, however, he opted to fight alongside him to withstand the Japanese invasion of China. He would go on to overthrow the nationalists and set up communism in his country with some terrible failures resulting in millions of deaths, and some notable successes.

AXIS POLITICAL LEADERS AND MILITARY GENERALS

Germany

Adolf Hitler

As the totalitarian leader of Nazi Germany, Hitler made some risky and brilliant strategic moves that saw him conquer almost all of Europe in such a short amount of time. By building up the military strength of his country, despite the treaty forbidding him to do so, and instilling a sense of pride in his people, he was able to mobilize Germany to war. But his ambition also saw him follow tactics that ultimately cost him the war, and in the end, he committed suicide in an underground bunker in Berlin (Noy, 2016).

Adolf Hitler

AMAZING FACTS

- *Hitler quit high school and tried to join the Vienna Academy for Fine Arts but was turned away, and without a mother and father at that stage, he was homeless and broke. He was also rejected by the Austrian Army for being "unfit, too weak, unable to bear arms" (Noy, 2016).*
- *He received the Iron Cross in WWI where he fought bravely and was wounded in action twice. In fact, Hitler could have died in WWI. In 1918, a British soldier, named Private Henry Tandey, was reported to have spared Hitler's life, when he later admitted he "couldn't shoot a wounded man" (Noy, 2016).*
- *Hitler married Eva Braun just before she took poison, and he shot himself in the head.*

Heinrich Himmler

Sharing the same ideas as Hitler, he got on very well with the Nazi leader, and as a result, rose to power with him. He remained loyal to Hitler and was given complete control of the SS, which ultimately oversaw the extermination of millions of people in the deadly concentration camps.

AMAZING FACTS

- *When it was clear that Germany would lose the war, Himmler secretly began peace negotiations until Hitler found out and stripped him of all his rank. He fled to Flensburg and contacted Eisenhower to work out a deal that would spare his own life but was rejected. Himmler finally disguised himself and tried escaping over the border but was caught and committed suicide by biting on a cyanide capsule hidden in his tooth (D-Day, n.d.).*

Hermann Göring

The second most powerful man in Nazi Germany, Göring's main role in the war was to oversee the Luftwaffe, the German air force (Beyer, 2013). A very powerful and wealthy man, he used his influence in the early days of the Nazi party to persuade the president to make Hitler chancellor. Göring was very involved in shifting the blame for the Reichstag fire and imprisoning any opponents.

During the beginning of the war, the Luftwaffe was very successful until the Battle of Britain where it suffered losing almost 2,000 aircraft (Beyer, 2013). Although it was a feared unit, the air force was unable to be very effective due to the loss of planes during battles.

When Hitler announced he would commit suicide to his generals, Göring asked if he could take the leader's place as head of government, but Hitler branded him a traitor and kicked him out of the Nazis. Göring was captured but took a cyanide capsule before he could be hanged as part of the sentence handed down for his crimes at the Nuremberg trials (Beyer, 2016).

AMAZING FACTS

- *During the failed Beer Hall Putsch in November 1923, Göring was shot in the groin and needed morphine for the pain. This started a lifelong addiction to the drug (Beyer, 2016).*

Erwin Rommel

Known as the "Desert Fox" because of his extensive role in North and East Africa during WW2, Rommel's brilliance as a strategist kept the Allies bogged down fighting battles across the continent. But it was his approach to war that won him the respect of his enemies, following the idea of "war without hate." Some reports say he died being shot in his car by RAF pilots, but others indicate that he was forced to commit suicide for his apparent part in an attempt to assassinate Hitler (D-Day, n.d.).

Joseph Goebbels

Goebbels was a key part of keeping the Nazis in power and the German people following Hitler's ideals. By using the media, he painted a glorified picture of the ruling party and their war effort, while at the same time, depicting the Jews to be the enemy. His skill at propaganda enabled him to remain one of the top leaders in the Nazi party and hide many of the atrocities that were being committed by officers in the SS.

In the end, he had his entire family poisoned before he and his wife also took cyanide capsules and died.

Japan

Admiral Hideki Tojo

The Prime Minister of Japan came from a long military background and was an aggressive proponent of war. It was his order that sent planes across the Pacific to attack Pearl Harbor in December 1941, and by 1944 had become commander-in-chief of all military (Noy, 2016). When it was clear that the war would be lost, Tojo resigned but was still held accountable and executed for the role he played.

Emperor Hirohito

As the next in line to rule after his father, Hirohito became Emperor of Japan in 1926 (D-Day, n.d.). He disagreed with his brother over whether to support Germany, but after Hitler's success in Europe, he joined the Axis Powers. Although he was not necessarily involved in military operations and decisions, Hirohito made many good suggestions to his generals.

He formally announced Japan's surrender soon after Hiroshima and Nagasaki were bombed on August 15, 1945 (D-Day, n.d.). General MacArthur forced him to denounce his godly status to the people and ensured he was stripped of all his lands and dominions.

Isoroku Yamamoto

Having spent some time in the United States, he saw the American Navy firsthand and argued that going to war with them would be a big mistake. However, when the pressure turned and war became inevitable, it was Yamamoto as commander of the Japanese fleet who came up with the plan of a surprise raid that could bomb ships in shallow water docks. In 1943, despite warnings of an ambush, he flew out to visit troops and boost their morale, but the convoy was shot down and Yamamoto was killed (Tovy, 2015).

Italy

Benito Mussolini

Mussolini was a bully from the age of 10 and was expelled and suspended for two separate stabbings of fellow students at school (History.com, 2018). As a former journalist encouraging violence in his newspapers, Mussolini went into politics. In 1922, with his armed supporters in black shirts, he marched into Rome to "take by the throat our miserable ruling class," and after the King dissolved the government, he became Italy's new Prime Minister (Brunies, 2021).

With the support of landowners, businessmen, and the King, Mussolini had powerful backing, but it was his brutal, violent handling of dissidents and opponents that scared many Italians into line. He used propaganda to build up a personality cult around himself.

Known as *"Il Duce,"* Mussolini was a terrible commander and made terrible strategic choices that cost the Italian army. In 1943, when it was clear they were losing the war, he was voted out by his own council, arrested, and sent away to an island. Hitler sent troops to free him and reinstate him as leader of North Italy, but this did not last long once Germans forces were overrun. He tried to escape with his lover, but they were captured, shot, and hung upside down in public view (History, 2018).

AMAZING FACTS

- *Hitler was inspired by Mussolini. He tried to copy his march into Rome, and even the Roman salute, and when they both met in 1938, Mussolini said that Hitler "had tears in his eyes" (Levin-Areddy, 2018).*

Victor Emmanuel III

The King took the throne after his father was assassinated in 1900 and held a very neutral stance when it came to politics. Although he disagreed with Mussolini's violent tactics, he happily accepted the extra titles of Emperor of Ethiopia and King of the Albanians when they had been conquered (Brunies, 2021). He seldom interfered except on the issue of entering the war which he forbade Mussolini to do until halfway through 1940.

After dismissing Mussolini as Prime Minister, the King continued the war effort while he negotiated a peace deal, but when it was signed, the Allies found it difficult to work with him (Brunies, 2019). The public had grown tired of the monarchy, and after the war, despite his attempts to put his son on the throne, a republic was declared, and the royals were exiled.

5

WORLD WAR 2 IN NUMBERS

Lasting over 6 years, WW2 had some battles that were over before they began, while others raged on, claiming lives, and changing the landscape forever. The war spread so far across the globe and involved so many different nationalities that the number of soldiers, weapons, deaths, and other statistics are quite astonishing. It demanded more people, more planes, ships, tanks, and a far higher cost than the one that was previously fought.

SHOCKING NUMBERS

- **194**

Countries involved in the war

- **15 million**

Deaths of soldiers in battle

- **45 million**

Deaths of civilians

- **16 million**

People left homeless

- **1 million**

Guns and artillery produced

- **4.5 million**

Military trucks produced

- **$1.3 trillion ($4 trillion equivalent today)**

Total cost of the war (Nielsen, 2019)

SURPRISING AMOUNTS

- **3,000**

The number of babies one midwife delivered at Auschwitz concentration camp during the Holocaust (Mighty, 2015).

- **3 to 22**

The number of sheets of toilet paper rationed to soldiers for each day—the British got 3, while the Americans got 22 (Mighty, 2015)!

- **100**

How many Japanese soldiers John McKinney fought off using only his M1 rifle. He killed 38 of them (Daniel, 2019)!

- **84**

The generals that Hitler had executed, mostly after he discovered they were plotting to kill him (Daniel, 2019).

- **1,400**

The number of missions Luftwaffe pilot Erich Hartmann flew in his Messerschmitt BF 109 with 352 kills (Tedeschi, 2020)!

6

TIMELINE OF THE WAR

Due to the scale of the war, it is easy to get lost in the different names of places, the number of soldiers involved, how many lived and died, and who won the battle in the end. Before getting into the specifics of each of the major confrontations, it is good to get an overview of WW2 from beginning to end —to put you in the picture before we dive down amongst the explosions and shooting.

Already having looked at the causes and reasons that the fighting began, stretching as far back as the signing of the Treaty of Versailles, our timeline will start at the very point that war was declared in 1939.

1939

Sept 1: Germany invaded Poland

Although events had been heating up before this, with Hitler building up his army and taking over territories in defiance of the

Treaty of Versailles, it was not until he actively targeted a country that Britain and France had sworn to protect that it became official. The nonaggression pact that had been signed a few weeks before between the Soviets and Germany meant that the two countries would not get in each other's way or turn on each other if they both assisted in crushing Poland.

Sept 3: Britain and France declared war on Germany

Other countries also declared war including Canada, Australia, New Zealand and South Africa. British troops are sent to France and the The Battle of the Atlantic began with the sinking of the British ship Athenia by a German U-Boat.

Sept 5: The United States declared neutrality

President Franklin D. Roosevelt promises Americans that they will not go to war.

Sept 5: The Soviet Union invaded Poland

Sept 27: Poland surrendered to Germany, with the country divided between Germany and the Soviet Union

Nov 30: The Soviets invaded Finland

Dec 13: The Battle of the River Plate, the first naval battle of the war, was fought.

1940

April–June: Hitler took over most of western Europe

After Poland fell, it seemed as though Germany stopped for 6 months, and some were calling it a "phony war," but it was just the beginning. On April 9th, the Nazis invaded Denmark and Norway, with the former country surrendering almost immediately (USHMM, 2018). Using his Blitzkrieg method, Hitler swept through Belgium, the Netherlands, and Luxembourg in quick succession.

At this time, Winston Churchill became Prime Minister of Britain after it became clear that Chamberlain's efforts amounted to nothing.

Germany invaded and subdued France in June.

June 4: The Allies suffered defeat at Dunkirk

June 10: Italy entered the war by attacking France

June–Aug: The Soviets occupied the Baltic states

Without attacking, Stalin engineered an overthrow of the Estonian, Latvian, and Lithuanian governments by encouraging communist uprisings.

July–Oct: The Battle of Britain

Hitler thought he could quickly bring Britain to its knees through attacks along the coast by plane, but the RAF withstood the onslaught, and after three months, the attack had to be called off (Nielsen, 2019).

Sept 7: The Blitz

German bombers began repeatedly dropping shells on England, targeting the main cities. For 57 nights in a row, London was hit.

The raids lasted 8 months (Gilbert, 2018).

Sept 13: Italy invaded Egypt

Sept 27: Tripartite Pact between Germany, Italy, and Japan

Oct 28: Italy invaded Greece

Nov: Hungary, Romania, and Slovakia joined the Axis Powers

1941

Feb: Germans assisted Italy in North Africa

Under the command of Erwin Rommel, the Nazis sent in their troops and armored divisions to reinforce the Italians who were struggling in the desert conditions. They had significant victories.

March 1: Bulgaria joined the Axis Powers

March: The United States sent supplies to Britain

While Roosevelt refused to enter the war at this stage, he convinced his government to help by supplying ammunition and other aid that was needed in the war effort.

April–June: Germany, Italy, and Hungary invaded Yugoslavia

June 22: Germany invaded the Soviet Union

Under the name of Operation Barbarossa, and with the help of Finland who were looking for payback, the Germans quickly conquered the Baltic states that Stalin had already taken and pushed through into Russia. The first phase of rounding up Jews in Russia to be exterminated began with death squads following troops and selecting those who would go to concentration camps. This would become part of the "Final Solution."

Sept 8: The Siege of Leningrad began

German troops cut off all supplies in the city in a siege that lasted for more than 2 years. As a result, more than 1 million people starved and died (Andrews, 2016).

Oct: The Germans pushed toward Moscow

Dec 6: The Soviets forced the Germans back

Dec 7: Japan bombed Pearl Harbor

The surprise attack on the U.S.-maintained port on the 7th of December forced America to declare war on Japan (USHMM, 2018). In retaliation, Germany, and Italy both threw their weight behind their ally and declared war on the United States.

1942

Jan 20: The "Final Solution" was implemented

Although death squads had already been busy in Russia rounding up and killing Jews, it was not until the Wannsee Conference took place that officials discussed the way forward on how to carry out the killing of so many people.

Jan: Japan conquered the Philippines and Manila

May 4–8: The Battle of the Coral Sea between U.S. and Japan

June 4–7: The Battle of Midway

One of the major turning points in WW2 was when the United States turned the battle into a victory and defeated the Japanese.

Aug 7: The Battle of Guadalcanal started

For the first time, the Allied forces were not countering an attack, but launching their own offensive against the Japanese in a series of coordinated strikes on certain islands in the Pacific.

Aug 23: The Battle of Stalingrad began

One of the fiercest and deadliest battles to be fought in WW2. It was another point where the course of the war shifted in the favor of the Allied Forces as Germany was forced to pull soldiers from other areas in Europe for reinforcement.

Oct 23–24: The Battle of El Alamein

British troops forced the Axis Powers to retreat quickly from Egypt back into Tunisia.

Nov 8: Operation Torch

North Africa was taken back by the Allies.

1943

Feb 2: Germans surrendered at Stalingrad

Mostly because of the harsh winter conditions and some harsh fighting, but also due to the Soviets surrounding the Germans and cutting off their supplies, the Nazis had to give in.

April 19: The Warsaw Ghetto Uprising

Thousands of Jews revolted against German forces, but the outcome was costly with 13,000 Jews being killed.

May 16–17: Operation Chastise

The RAF's "Dambuster" plan to destroy dams that were crucial to Germany's war effort.

July–Aug: The Battle of Kursk

The largest tank battle in history was launched by the Germans but was very quickly cut off by the Soviets.

July 25: Mussolini was deposed

Sept 8: Italy surrendered

The government surrendered to the Allies, but Germany invaded the north of the country, and rescued Mussolini.

Oct: Allies retook Italy

Nov 28: The Big Three met

Roosevelt, Churchill, and Stalin met for the first time at the Tehran Conference and discussed the direction for the rest of the war.

1944

Jan: The Siege of Leningrad ended

Feb 20–25: Big Week

The U.S. Air Force and RAF carried out a series of raids against the Luftwaffe and lured them into combat where they could be damaged. It was also called Operation Argument and was critical in achieving air superiority before the invasion of D-Day (Wueschner, 2019).

June 6: D-Day

U.S., Canadian, and British troops landed on the beaches of Normandy, the largest seaborne invasion. Despite heavy losses against the Germans, it was a highly successful attack and was the start of the liberation of Europe.

Aug 25: The Allies entered the French capital city

Sept 17–27: Operation Market Garden

One of the biggest failures for the Allies, the plan was to push through the Netherlands creating a pathway to a bridgehead over the Rhine River into Germany. But German forces stopped them from taking the key bridges they needed.

Dec 16: The Battle of the Bulge

Hitler's last attempt to counterattack, split the Allied army, and reconquer Belgium, took place in the Ardennes Forest. At first, the U.S. troops struggled in the conditions, but instead of surrendering, pushed through and forced the Germans to retreat into their own country.

1945

Jan 12: The East Prussian Offensive

The Soviets began to move through toward Germany, freed Warsaw and Krakow in Poland, and Budapest in Hungary. In the process, they liberated the Auschwitz concentration camp on January 27.

Feb–Mar: The Battle of Iwo Jima

Apr 16: Soviets surround Berlin

Apr 28: Mussolini was killed

Apr 29: Dachau concentration camp was liberated

Apr 30: Hitler committed suicide

May 7: Germany surrendered

In a red schoolhouse in France, which was Eisenhower's headquarters, Germany formally surrendered. The armistice came into effect the next day, the 8th, and is now celebrated as V-E Day (Victory in Europe).

Aug 6: Little Boy was dropped on Hiroshima

After the first atomic bomb exploded, killing 140,000 people, there was no response from Japan.

Aug 9: Fat Man was dropped on Nagasaki

A second atomic bomb was dropped, hitting the Japanese city, and killing 74,000.

Sept 2: Japan surrendered

After agreeing in principle on August 12, Japan only formally surrendered in September, marking the end of WW2.

7

MAJOR EVENTS AND BATTLES—1939

There was no massive explosion or deadly battle that began WW2. Everything started very slowly, mainly because the British were treading softly around Hitler as he took land bit by bit. Armies were taking time to build up their forces in case of war, but for certain politicians, there was still talk of peace, and a belief that any kind of confrontation could be avoided.

This was the furthest thing from Hitler's mind! His book, *Mein Kampf*, written in 1925 painted a clear picture of his intentions (1999): *"He who would live must fight. He who doesn't wish to fight in this world, where permanent struggle is the law of life, has not the right to exist."*

But the aspirations of the Nazi leader were never just to build up Germany, it was always to extend the borders, so the Aryan race could have *"Lebensraum"* (living space). This meant expanding—that meant war!

INVASION OF POLAND

The invasion began before troops started moving into Poland. A nonaggression pact between the Soviets and the Germans paved the way for an attack that would not upset these two countries. Hitler agreed not to interfere with Stalin pushing into the Baltic states, and Russia would assist in the invasion. As part of the deal, both nations would get a split of Poland.

With this in place, Poland was ready to be taken. The only issue Hitler had not counted on was that Britain would finally act on its threat to protect those borders.

September 1–October 6

To justify the invasion, the Nazis accused Poland of persecuting Germans who were living there, and that the country had been planning to attack Germany.

With over 9,000 artillery, 2,750 tanks, 2,000 aircraft, and 1.5 million soldiers, the Germans broke through any Polish defenses in the north and south (Browne, 2018). They quickly moved in and surrounded Warsaw, the capital city, where they began to inflict heavy bombing on it.

Poland was slow to mobilize its army, and it had outdated guns and equipment compared with the modern German artillery. It also suffered the loss of many of their planes as the Luftwaffe had targeted them in the first days of the attack. The Polish army put up a brave defense, but with the Soviets entering from the east, they faced an impossible situation. The war was over in a few weeks. Unfortunately, 66,000 Polish soldiers died, 133,000 were wounded, and 787,000 were taken captive (Browne, 2018).

Poland surrendered on September 28 and remained under the Nazis until close to the end of WW2.

Although Britain and France declared war as a result, neither of them was ready to engage in one. There was no Polish government left to free, so instead of rushing in, the war cooled down for six months before the next major offensive.

AMAZING FACTS

- *After Germany's invasion of Poland, the next six months of the war became known as the "Phony War" because there was almost no fighting in Europe. In Germany, this period was known as the Sitzkrieg ("Sitting War").*

EVACUATION OF CHILDREN IN BRITAIN

Realizing war had indeed begun, Britain took action. Instead of marching its soldiers into Poland, it focused on securing its citizens from an attack from the German Luftwaffe on Britain itself. It began a mass evacuation of children into areas that were not seen as major targets.

September 1–3

Under the name of Operation Pied Piper, 1.5 million children were removed from their parents and sent to rural communities far from the cities (The History Press, 2019). Most of these were put on trains headed for the countryside, while some boarded ships that sailed from the River Thames to other ports in Britain. Some mothers and pregnant women were included in the move.

It was not compulsory, but it was strongly advised. Each child had specific luggage that they had to take including a gas mask. They were given labels to wear as they were taken to safer areas in Britain. The emotional trauma for some was huge, while others had no idea what was taking place. Along with their items, every child received a postcard that they could send back home once they had reached their destination (The History Press, 2019).

Living in other people's homes was strange, and some children did not enjoy it, some even ran away. Others found it eye-opening as they saw farm animals and ate vegetables from the land.

When the war was over in 1945, returning home after so many years was not an easy process as some children had lost their homes and families, or felt emotionally distant from their parents (The History Press, 2019).

BATTLE OF THE ATLANTIC

While Hitler was invading Poland, and the world's eyes were focused on what he was going to do next, other incidents were taking place that are often overlooked by many in the history of WW2. The stand-off between German U-boats, and the importance of the shipping lanes between America and Europe remains a critical part of the war's timeline.

September 3, 1939–May 7, 1945

The German submarine division, known as U-boats, played a vital role in the war as the British and U.S. Navies struggled with ongoing attacks, not just on military vessels, but on merchant ships, and even passenger liners. The idea was that if Germany could control the waters between America and England, it would stop any supplies of weapons or goods that were desperately needed to fight a war against the Nazis.

On September 3, 1939, a British passenger liner called the *SS Athenia* on its way from Glasgow to Montreal was hit by a torpedo from a U-boat killing 112 people on board, 3/4 of whom were women and children. Soon afterwards all merchant ships were armed, had to travel in convoy, and given permission to ram into any German vessels if they needed to. Despite being the first to attack, General Admiral Karl Donitz, who oversaw the U-boat fleet did not appreciate these methods and gave his men an "open-attack" policy on all Allied merchant ships (SecondWorldWarHistory, 2022).

In the first four months of deploying the submarines, 100 vessels were sunk; in 1941, almost 500 were lost; and in 1942, over 1,000 ships were destroyed despite all the safety measures that were put in place to counter these attacks (SecondWorldWar-History, 2022). But by 1943, tactics in the Allied Navy had improved and along with the RAF pinpointing the U-boats from the air, the Germans' tight grip on the Atlantic had disappeared.

Carrier Capsizing

WINTER WAR

The mistrust between Finland and the Soviets started shortly after WWI. Worried that Russia would attack them, they tried to enter an alliance with Estonia, Latvia, and Poland, but this did not happen. So, in 1932, the Finnish-Soviet nonaggression pact was signed (Encyclopedia Britannica, 2018c). But Stalin was worried about Germany's expansion and looked to expand his borders to give himself more safety in case the Nazis attacked. He also wanted the use of a Naval base, but his proposals for an exchange of land were refused.

November 30, 1939–March 12, 1940

No sooner had Poland fallen than Stalin turned his attention to Finland. Breaking the pact they had signed, he sent about 1 million troops to attack many different fronts (Encyclopedia Britannica, 2018c). But the Red Army hardly made any progress. The winter was freezing, and the Russians were not used to fighting in those weather conditions. Added to this, Stalin's purge where he got rid of any opponents to his government left the army in disarray. It looked like defeat.

One unit of Soviet soldiers that were surrounded sent out a message: *"We are dying, please pay our March wages to our families. Tell everyone that we died as heroes… we did not surrender"* (Chapple, 2019).

But in February 1940, the Soviets began using heavy military bombardments that broke open the Finnish resistance and allowed troops to push through. After all their valiant fighting, the Finns made peace signing the Treaty of Moscow that agreed to Stalin's terms and ended the Russo-Finnish or Winter War (Encyclopedia Britannica, 2018c). Over 25,000 Finns died in the fighting compared to the massive 126,875 soldiers that the Soviets lost (Chapple, 2019).

Later, Finland allowed German soldiers to travel through their country when they were going to attack the Soviets, and even joined in the fighting to secure their land back from Stalin. This proved to be a disastrous decision for them as they suffered alongside the Nazis in a long, drawn-out push into Russia that ultimately backfired.

BATTLE OF THE RIVER PLATE

During the period between the invasion of Poland and Hitler's invading the rest of Europe, there were a few months when it seemed as though the war had stopped, and many called it a "phony war." But across the Atlantic waters, there was much activity as U-boats and German warships created havoc for Allied sea transport.

Hans Langsdorff was in command of the *KMS Admiral Graf Spee*, a German warship armed with six 11-inch guns and with a top speed of 28 knots. The British nicknamed them "pocket battleships" because of their size. She became a headache to the Allies as Langsdorff took her on a sinking spree, sending eight merchant ships to the bottom of the sea between September and December (IWM, 2022b). As a result, a large contingent was put together to hunt down the culprit.

Twenty-three warships were split into seven groups, all tasked with finding the *Graf Spee*. During this time, Langsdorff continued his destruction and claimed three more ships before heading off to the busy seas of the River Plate in South America (IWM, 2022b).

December 13

Commodore Henry Harwood oversaw one of these groups, and by using his calculations and estimations, he worked out where Langsdorff had gone. Armed with three ships, the large *HMS*

Exeter, the smaller *HMS Ajax,* and *HMS Achilles,* they cornered the *Graf Spee* (IWM, 2022b).

But the experience of Langsdorff showed as he focused all his guns on the heavy cruiser. In the process, he destroyed the *Exeter's* guns and set her on fire, forcing her to retreat to safety. The *Ajax* took the next barrage of hits, and she lost two of her turrets. Seeing a gap, Langsdorff escaped into the Port of Montevideo in Uruguay while Harwood kept watch.

In international law, a ship can only stay in a neutral port for 24 hours, but the *Graf Spee* remained there for 72 hours (IWM, 2022b). Seeing no way out, and not wishing to face the might of the extra ships that had gathered waiting for him, Langsdorff sank his own ship. The *Graf Spee* was no more, and the Allies recorded a victory for themselves.

8

MAJOR EVENTS AND BATTLES—1940

INVASION OF NORWAY

Up until this point, the Axis and Allied troops had not engaged in combat. All the fighting had been through other countries, or from warships and U-boats, but Norway marked the first real face-to-face encounter.

Norway had remained neutral so far and had been hoping to stay out of the conflict brewing between Britain and the Nazis. Germany was looking for a strategic Naval base from which it could launch attacks against the British in the North Sea as well as secure much-needed iron ore through Sweden. After six months of no ground activity from the Nazis, this sparked the beginning of the German's European offensive.

April 9

Although Norway was not very well armed, Germany still launched a full-scale attack with several surprise invasions that ended in the capital city and main ports being quickly captured. A mass of 10,000 troops marched into Oslo putting an end to most Norwegian resistance (IWM, 2018). At the same time, German forces also occupied Copenhagen in Denmark.

Allied forces entered Norway on April 14 to intervene but were met with a bolstered force of 25,000 Nazis. Without the proper equipment, the Allies could not match the efficiency of the Germans, and by May 2, they had evacuated all their troops from the country (IWM, 2018).

At sea though, the Germans suffered major setbacks when their brand-new warship *Blücher* was hit by Norwegian coastal guns and sunk (IWM, 2018). When encountering the British Navy, there were a few miscalculations and disastrous decisions that ended in German ships being hit, sunk, or run aground, which proved to be costly later when they could not fully assist at Dunkirk or invading Britain (IWM, 2018).

AMAZING FACTS

- *Food rationing of butter, bacon and sugar in Britain, began in January 1940. Egg rationing was set at one egg per person per week (if available) and one packet of dried egg per person each month. Even the Queen's coronation cake in 1952 was made from rationed ingredients. Rationing didn't end in Britain until July 4, 1954, 4 years later than in Germany.*

THE BATTLE OF FRANCE

The Allies were still planning and thinking as they had done in WWI which was a trench war. The objective in those days was to dig in and hold the line. But they were completely unprepared for the Germans' modern strategy of war—the Blitzkrieg! Using tanks, artillery, and infantry in a combined offensive, the Nazis threw the enemy into chaos, punching through their defense, and overwhelming them with speed.

Europe fell in six weeks to what was becoming known as the "German War Machine."

May 10–June 25

Beginning in the Netherlands, Belgium, and Luxembourg, Hitler sent his troops in with air and ground attacks that wrecked any defensive lines that had been set to withstand them. The pace of the attacks stunned the Dutch and Belgians, and within a matter of days, all the Low Countries had been taken.

With the Allies focusing on the action in the north, German Panzer tanks swept around for a surprise breakthrough. France was under the impression that they would be attacked the same way they had in the previous war. They put all their efforts into strengthening the Maginot Line along the border and were caught off guard when the Germans broke through the Ardennes Forest, and bypassed any major resistance (Correll, 2018).

Lt. Gen. Heinz Guderian, Germany's best tank officer at the time, was convinced that speed would win them the advantage, and once he and Rommel's divisions had crossed the Meuse River, they raced into France before anyone had an idea of what was going on (Correll, 2018). With the French forces split and surrounded, there was no way they could properly combat the invasion.

On May 15, French Premier Paul Reynaud told Churchill on the phone, "*We have been defeated; we have lost the battle*" (Correll, 2018). Although a few minor confrontations still occurred, the battle was already over, and Paris was left open for the Germans to walk straight in with an armistice being signed in June.

Even though it was swift, the Germans suffered the loss of 27,074 men and many tanks and planes in the process, while

90,000 French soldiers died (Correll, 2018). Within six weeks of the invasion of Norway, only Britain was left standing against the Nazis.

AMAZING FACTS

- *To add insult to France's injury, Adolf Hitler ordered the French surrender to be signed in the same railway car where the humiliating German surrender to France was signed at the end World War I, a decade earlier.*

DUNKIRK

Although it's officially part of the Battle of France, what happened at Dunkirk on the French coast stands on its own as a military story that's filled with incredible events.

As German forces swept through France, cutting off communication, supplies, and any real chance of retaliation, around 400,000 Allied soldiers had been cornered and ended up stuck at Dunkirk with no way out. The Panzer tanks had raced up ahead but stopped before reaching the beach. They had been told to stop by Hitler—the reason for this is still not known.

May 26–June 3

Called Operation Dynamo, it was a rescue effort that was initially estimated at only being able to save 45,000 of the stranded men (Boissoneault, 2017). With the Luftwaffe knocking out any of the port facilities and dropping bombs across the beach and onto ships waiting to fetch men, it quickly became a war zone.

Soldiers had to stand in lines in the water or on the eastern pier (mole) that jutted out into the sea where boats could fetch them.

All the while, German planes were trying to pick them off as RAF fighters tried to force the Luftwaffe back.

The response to help came in the form of the "little ships." Over and above those recruited by the army, civilian ships of every size and shape made their way out to help ferry the men to safety. Some made the journey across the Channel more than once over the following days until 338,226 people were back in England (Boissoneault, 2017).

Although it was a rescue mission, it was seen as a morale booster, especially because most of those that were rescued ended up back in Europe to help fight the Nazis. It inspired Churchill to make one of his most well-known speeches on June 4 (Hansard, 2018):

> *We shall go on to the end, we shall fight in France, we shall fight on the seas and oceans, we shall fight with growing confidence, and growing strength in the air, we shall defend our island, whatever the cost may be. We shall fight on the beaches, we shall fight on the landing grounds, we shall fight in the fields, and in the streets, we shall fight in the hills; we shall never surrender.*

THE BATTLE OF BRITAIN

The only country left that remained against Hitler was Britain. He had not made any plans to invade as he expected the British to discuss peace options rather than fight. When this did not happen, he came up with Operation Sea Lion, a strategy to prepare the way for soldiers to land on the island, even though the Germans were not fully prepared for it. The Luftwaffe would begin by attacking Naval vessels, and key military points on the coastline, and engaging with the RAF.

July 10–October 31

With almost four times more planes than the British, the Luftwaffe began targeting Navy vessels, then turned its attention to taking out radar stations and aircraft factories. The fighting was intense between both countries, but by the end of August, the Nazis had lost 600 aircraft to the RAF's 260 (Encyclopedia Britannica, 2019).

77th Squadron Royal Air Force

On August 24th, German pilots strayed off course, bombing London by mistake, that resulted in the RAF retaliating by hitting Berlin (Encyclopedia Britannica, 2019). Hitler then shifted his attention to focus entirely on London, but by that time, the Luftwaffe had suffered devastating losses, and on September 7, Operation Sea Lion had been scrapped by Hitler. By the end of October, it was clear that the RAF was too strong, and Germany pulled back.

The defeat of the Luftwaffe had a serious impact later in WW2 as their ability to maintain any kind of control over the Allied forces in the air had been destroyed.

AMAZING FACTS

- *Many of the pilots in the Royal Air Force were from other countries such as Poland, Czechoslovakia, Canada, Australia, and South Africa. A Polish fighter squadron shot down the most German planes together during the war—126 (Andrews, 2015).*
- *Sgt. Ray Holmes had no more ammunition when he saw a German bomber heading straight for Buckingham Palace, so he rammed into it with his wing, sending both aircraft crashing off-course, and saving the royal residence (Andrews, 2015).*
- *Fearing a German invasion, all road signs in Britain were removed, to confuse invading troops and possible German spies (National Army Museum, 2017).*

THE BLITZ

Although this falls within the Battle of Britain, it stands out as a significant event. The struggle for supremacy in the air had mainly been focused on military structures and enemy aircraft, but by September, civilians became targets.

September 7, 1940–May 11, 1941

Black Saturday marked the first wave of 350 bombers that unleashed explosives on London resulting in 450 fatalities and over 1,500 people injured (Gilbert, 2018a). Mainly the east of the city was hit as this is where most industrial buildings and docks were located. For 57 consecutive nights, the Luftwaffe flew out across London, raining down bombs wherever they thought the targets were located. Since most of the raids took place at night, it was difficult to pinpoint, and the collateral damage suffered by civilians was massive.

Fireman tackling fires in the aftermath of a German raid.

A total blackout was used along with warning sirens, and people were instructed to find shelter. Many people used the underground stations to hide from the shelling, sometimes over 100,000 a night. Another method employed, in trying to prevent the aircraft from flying too low and having good aim at their targets, was using barrage balloons—large, inflatable, oval balloons that forced the Germans up higher to avoid hitting them.

Hitler's intention was not just to take out key targets, but to break the spirit of the British people, and pressure the government to surrender. Even though there was much death and destruction, the citizens of London persevered and proved Hitler wrong. One of the key phrases used to encourage and inspire them is still used today (Gilbert, 2018a):

"Keep calm and carry on."

After eight months, 43,000 civilians had lost their lives in the bombings, and over 1 million houses and flats were destroyed, leaving 1/6 of the population without homes (Gilbert, 2018a). Despite the losses, the country still stood, and the Blitz turned out to be a waste of strategic maneuvers by the Germans.

Later the Allies sent their own bombers across parts of Germany with devastating effects on the cities they hit as well as the morale of the people.

AMAZING FACTS

- *The city of Coventry had so many explosives dropped on it on November 14, 1940, that the smell of burning buildings reached up to the pilots of the German bombers flying overhead (Bancroft, 2022).*
- *In Operation Columba, the British parachuted over 16,000 homing pigeons into occupied Europe, each carrying some paper and a pencil to try and gain intelligence on the enemy. The Germans responded by punishing people with the death penalty if they didn't hand the pigeons in. They also trained hawks to kill the pigeons. The pigeons were considered so important that MI5 (British Intelligence Service) set up the Falcon Destruction Unit to kill any enemy birds attacking their pigeons. Only one in ten returned alive, but some provided crucial information.*

9

MAJOR EVENTS AND BATTLES—1941

OPERATION BARBAROSSA

Hitler had reached as far west as he could go in Europe. Britain still withstood him despite his attempts to subdue the country, but he realized that it was time to put into action what he had planned to do all along—invade the Soviet Union. He had promised the German people "*Lebensraum,*" and Russia would provide that. In addition, there were some key military points that Hitler wanted to have control of.

Even though his army was far outnumbered, and the Germans had less firepower than the Soviets, Hitler believed that the element of force and speed would be enough.

June 22, 1941–January 7, 1942

Three million men, 3,000 tanks, 7,000 pieces of artillery, and 2,500 aircraft assembled ready to invade Russia, the biggest in history (Royde-Smith, 2018). They were divided into three groups that would attack from the left, the right, and the main force through the center. It took the Soviets by surprise, leaving them in confusion as the Panzer divisions blew their way through any resistance.

It proved harder than the French offensive because of the large numbers of Soviet troops they had to take prisoner as well as the resistance they met with, and the scorched earth policy where the Russians burned everything, leaving no provisions for the Germans to pick up (Royde-Smith, 2018). But with the speed that the Nazis moved, pushed them within 200 miles of Moscow, where the army came to a halt.

Hitler and his generals spent precious time arguing about the direction to take from there. This cost the Germans. Instead of charging into Moscow, Hitler turned his attention to Ukraine for its resources, and by the end of July, Kiev had been taken (Royde-Smith, 2018). By the end of September, over 500,000 men had been captured, partly because Stalin refused to withdraw any of them, ordering them to stand and fight.

The Germans had pushed hard and far and were exhausted and hungry. Added to this problem was that the Russian winter was closing in fast, causing even more problems. Instead of attacking Leningrad, Hitler ordered his men to surround it and wait. An attempt was made to infiltrate Moscow, but the tanks struggled in the snow, there were not enough supplies of fuel and ammunition, and the men froze. The number of casualties in Hitler's army up until the end of November had reached 730,000 (Royde-Smith, 2018). On top of this, a fierce counterattack from the Soviets damaged the German lines with fresh reinforcements pouring in from the outlying areas. The invasion eventually stalled and proved to be a major setback for the Nazi war plan.

However, Operation Barbarossa was not just about conquering cities and taking land, it soon became a war of horror and cruelty. Although it was officially forbidden to kill those who surrendered, it was encouraged by the German commanders. Instead of taking prisoners, both the Germans and the Soviets began killing those soldiers, sometimes in very barbaric ways. About 2.8 million Soviet POWS were murdered by their Nazi captors (Carter, 2018). The hatred that had been drummed into both sides for each other spilled out across Russia as towns were looted, people murdered, and women raped.

The Jews were especially targeted, and over 1.5 million were killed (Yadvashem, 2019).

AMAZING FACTS

- *Britain decoded German messages that they had intercepted about an attack that was about to take place on Russia. Winston Churchill then warned Stalin about the impending invasion, but the Soviet leader thought the British were just trying to break up the alliance he had with Germany, so he ignored it (Knighton, 2017).*
- *The Germans used over 600,000 horses in the invasion of the Soviet Union.*
- *Four of every five German soldiers killed in the war died on the Eastern front.*

SIEGE OF LENINGRAD

Hitler's strategic brilliance in sweeping through Europe faltered when he turned toward Russia. He stuck to some ideas that cost him dearly, but he also changed his mind when he should have followed the initial plan. One of these moments occurred when his troops arrived at Leningrad, the birthplace of communism, a symbol that Hitler wanted to get rid of.

September 8, 1941–January 27, 1944

Under the command of General Field Marshal Wilhelm Ritter von Leeb, 500,000 Germans marched onto Leningrad (now called St. Petersburg) with orders to conquer it by July 21 (Andrews, 2016). But this did not happen. Once the first push into Russia had been achieved, things began to slow down as commanders argued, and the winter set in. Hitler decided not to risk losing lots of soldiers in street battles and chose to blockade the city instead. It became the longest siege of a city in modern history (Wagner, 2016).

The citizens of Leningrad had already begun reinforcing their fortifications, and by November, the Germans had cut off every rail and supply line to the city. Hitler told von Leeb not to accept any surrender as they did not have enough food for prisoners (Andrews, 2016). He wanted them to starve to death.

The other directive was to level Leningrad to the ground by continual bombing. The Luftwaffe made regular passes over the city dropping bombs that destroyed supplies along with homes and people. In total, 75,000 bombs fell on Leningrad over the course of the siege (Andrews, 2016).

But it was the lack of food that killed most of the inhabitants. Rations of bread amounted to about 6 slices of bread per day for workers or 3 for children and the elderly. As winter gripped the region, people began to starve, and up to 100,000 died every month. People began to eat anything that could sustain them; wallpaper, leather, dogs and cats, and even each other (Andrews, 2016)! The only supplies trickled in through a gap along Lake Ladoga, but even this was not nearly enough. Furniture and books were burned to keep warm as temperatures dropped.

Of the 2.5 million people that were stuck in Leningrad from the beginning of the siege, almost half of them died. But just as the citizens of Britain endured their terror during the bombing of

London, the Russians picked themselves up and continued. In early 1942, after the harsh winter, they cleaned up rubble, buried the dead, planted gardens, and even held a symphonic concert with the loudspeakers pointed out toward their enemies (Andrews, 2016).

At the beginning of 1943, the Soviet Army had taken back a small piece of land and engineered a rail link that could supply food back into Leningrad. A year later, after almost 900 days, the Germans were forced to retreat, and the city was opened again on January 27, 1944.

AMAZING FACTS

- *The Siege of Leningrad resulted in more Russian deaths (military and civilian) than the United States and Britain sustained (combined) in all of WW2.*

ATTACK ON PEARL HARBOR

The Japanese had made it clear that they wanted to expand the empire. By pushing into China, it had broken the Treaty of Versailles, and defied the League of Nations. But this was not enough. As an empire, it wanted control of the Pacific Islands, and the only thing that stood in its way was the American Navy. All it needed was to neutralize that threat.

December 7

There was already tension between Japan and America as the United States was supporting the Chinese against the Imperial invasion. By the time the Tripartite Pact was signed, all commercial and financial relations had been cut. Talks about peace continued right up until the day Pearl Harbor was bombed, but the order for the attack had been given over a month before.

Japanese Adm. Yamamoto Isoroku had spent much time planning the attack, even though he had warned his superiors that such an act would stir up the revenge of the U.S. forces. Two weeks before the assault, a large fleet was stationed to the north of Hawaii: 6 aircraft carriers, 2 battleships, 3 cruisers, and 11 destroyers. The main contingent of this was in the form of 360 planes that would unleash their explosives on the harbor (Ray, 2020b).

There had been several warnings that should have put the U.S. base on high alert, but these were either not taken seriously, or did not have enough evidence for them to be acted upon. In the minds of the American commanders, the strike would happen at sea and not in the harbor itself. When Washington realized on December 7 that something was about to happen, it was too late. Even at Pearl Harbor, the sighting of a Japanese submarine, and a large flight of planes on radar was not enough to convince them.

At 7:55 a.m. the first dive-bomber was seen, followed by 200 more planes that targeted the airfields around the base. The U.S. forces were totally unprepared. More than 300 of their aircraft were wiped out. But the biggest casualties were the large ships docked in the harbor. The *USS Arizona* took a direct hit and exploded sending her to the bottom with over 1,000 men still inside. The *USS Oklahoma* suffered too, as torpedoes struck, causing her to capsize (Ray, 2020b).

Pearl Harbor

Less than two hours later, every ship was damaged, and almost 2,500 people had been killed. Although it was a significant success, the Japanese had failed in their attempt to completely sabotage the U.S. Navy. Most of the important vessels were out at sea at that moment, and would be at full strength for later reprisals on Japan.

America could no longer remain neutral, and the next day it declared war on Japan. It also marked one of Roosevelt's most famous sentences as he spoke about the attack on Pearl Harbor (AOP, 2016):

"A date which will live in infamy."

AMAZING FACTS

- *The Japanese ships all kept radio silence up until the attack when the words "Tora! Tora! Tora!" (Tiger! Tiger! Tiger!) were broadcast as a code that meant the invasion was successful (AOP, 2016).*
- *Within 30 days after the attack on Pearl Harbor, 134,000 Americans had signed up to be part of the military. Fifty million would eventually be employed in some way or another as part of the war effort (Pearl Harbor Tours Blog, 2018).*

10

MAJOR EVENTS AND BATTLES—1942

INTERNMENT STARTS IN AMERICA

The surprise attack on Pearl Harbor sparked fear and suspicion among Americans, especially toward anyone with Japanese ancestry. No one was sure which side these *foreigners* were on, even if they had been in the United States their whole lives. The only way the government could deal with this was to pass a law to detain anyone who might be a threat.

February 19, 1942–December 18, 1944

Executive Order 9066 was a very broad instruction to deal with civilians who were a military threat. It did not specify any ethnic group, but the focus was mainly on Japanese Americans. They were first given a curfew, then the opportunity to evacuate from certain areas, and finally, forced removal or detention. None of these were allowed to serve in the army (National Archives, 2017).

Between March and August, almost 120,000 people were moved to relocation centers where they would be detained until the end of the war. Over half of these were legitimate U.S. citizens. Conditions in the camps were basic, often consisting of tar-papered barracks with flimsy partitions for privacy. School and other social engagements carried on within these confines (National Archives, 2017).

In 1988, U.S. President Reagan issued an official apology for the internment, acknowledging that it was racist (National Archives, 2017).

AMAZING FACTS

- *One of the most highly decorated U.S. Army units that fought in Europe in 1944 were the 442nd Regimental Combat Team that was made up entirely of 14,000 Japanese Americans (National Archives, 2017).*

BOMBING OF COLOGNE

Despite the Luftwaffe's superiority in the skies over Europe, the RAF still had to attempt ways to knock out key installations belonging to the German forces. One of the ways to do this was to conduct attacks with a concentrated number of bombers flying in and out. The raids on Cologne were one of their successes.

May 30–31

As an important railway junction, and a manufacturing city, Cologne was the perfect target to instill large-scale damage. Although the first bombing took place on May 12 and many more after it, Operation Millennium was so devastating because it consisted of 1,046 bombers to cause as much damage as possible in a short window of time (Trethewey, 1992). In one night, almost

600 acres of Cologne were flattened, with most of the central city gone.

Cologne Bombing

The main idea of the raid was to devastate the city and break the people's morale much like Hitler had tried during the Blitz. But instead, their spirit held, maybe because of the sight of the Cathedral still standing after the bombings. Miraculously, the twin spires of the holy building stood high in the sky. Cologne would be hit with over 20,000 tons of explosives throughout the war, but by the end of 1945, much of the population had returned to help clean and rebuild (Trethewey, 1992).

BATTLE OF MIDWAY

Yamamoto's prediction was correct. Six months after waking the "sleeping giant" at Pearl Harbor, the Japanese would feel the full consequences. Midway was a strategic island that would have allowed Japan to control the Pacific and launch attacks from there. The battle was mostly fought by aircraft and was one of the first successful contacts the Americans had that would signal a turning point in WW2 against its enemy.

June 3–7

The victory at Midway was mainly due to codebreakers. Cryptanalysts had been hard at work trying to decipher the Japanese messages and had identified that the Japanese were targeting a place known only as "AF." The American base at Midway sent out false communication that there was no fresh water there, and soon after a Japanese message came through confirming "AF" had water problems. They knew where it would happen, and soon after cracked the code to give them the date of June 4 or 5 (National WW2 Museum, 1999).

Japan's initial attack was successful as they damaged the base at Midway, but what they were not expecting was an extra U.S. Naval force that had been hidden until that point. Aircraft from the U.S. carriers launched attacks on the Japanese ships, and after numerous attempts, located and caused extensive damage to three: *Akagi, Kaga,* and *Soryu* (National WW2 Museum, 1999).

The last of the main ships, the *Hiryu,* managed to send planes that hit the USS *Yorktown*. But by the afternoon, the Americans had another wave of aircraft that put the *Hiryu* out of action. There was much fighting over the next two days, but with Japan's carriers disabled, they were finally forced to retreat.

Japanese losses amounted to over 3,000 men, four carriers, and more than 300 planes compared to the United States' 362 men, one carrier, a destroyer, and 140 aircraft. The Americans would push forward in their "island hopping" campaign that successfully forced the Japanese back (National WW2 Museum, 1999).

BATTLE OF STALINGRAD

Stalingrad was a key city. It had faced a battle over 20 years before, in the Russian Civil War, when it was called Tsaritsyn because of its strategic position along the Volga River. At that time, Josef Stalin was part of the Bolshevik victory. But in 1942, the Soviets found their backs against the wall as the Germans raced into Russia with lightning speed. While a third of the army turned down into Ukraine, another division attempted to take Moscow. The remaining force was sent to destroy Stalingrad, but instead of victory, the Nazis would face the bloodiest battle in the whole of WW2.

August 23, 1942–February 2, 1943

The Wehrmacht (German army) arrived at Stalingrad, and immediately began a massive artillery attack assisted by Luftwaffe flying overhead, dropping bombs. The Red Army held off the Nazis for a while, but they suffered huge losses. Soon the city was turned to rubble with almost every building knocked down by explosions. The Germans controlled almost all of Stalingrad, except for a pocket of resistance that held the northern part of the city.

They thought that the Soviets were collapsing, but Hitler underestimated the number of reinforcements, and the depth of his enemy's resources. Instead of being on their last legs, they surged. Rather than run, they fought back.

Instead of turning and retreating, the Soviets remained. Stalin had issued Order No. 227 which was summed up in the words (Merridale, 2011):

"Not a step back!"

Instead of printed posters and pamphlets, the slogan was

passed throughout the country by word-of-mouth until every citizen and soldier knew their duty. Anyone who deserted their post was shot.

By this stage, the Wehrmacht was struggling to get food through its stretched-out supply lines, the winter had proved harsh, and many of the men were exhausted from the long distances they had moved over so quickly in their Blitzkrieg maneuvers. Added to this, they were not used to urban fighting. Reducing the city to debris now proved to be an obstacle as they struggled to move freely or to locate the enemy.

The Soviets used tunnels, sewers, and rubble to launch devastating attacks on the Germans. In a counterattack, the Red Army initiated Operation Uranus that was designed to flank the opponent on either side and surround them. On November 23, the Germans were trapped in the city they had taken, but Hitler refused to let the 300,000 men retreat. But even this did not finish the Wehrmacht who fought back despite being tired and weak (Trouillard, 2022).

Another attack came in January of the following year, and the Nazis finally surrendered at the end of the month. After 200 days of brutal fighting, the battle was over having claimed 2 million lives from both sides: soldiers, and civilians (Trouillard, 2022).

AMAZING FACTS

- *A building that the Germans tried to take for months on the Volga River became known as Pavlov's house. When the officers of Yakov Pavlov's platoon were killed, he took over and secured the house with landmines, barbed wire, and a secret trench for receiving supplies and messages. Despite being outnumbered, the house never fell into German hands, and Pavlov survived the war (Beyer, 2022b).*

- *The first defenders of Stalingrad were women from the 1077th Anti-Aircraft Regiment. Most were teenage girls, just out of school, who held off the German advance for two days. When their position was finally overrun by the overwhelming German assault, the Germans were surprised to find they had been fighting girls and described their defense as "tenacious."*

BATTLE OF GUADALCANAL

Up until now, the United States had only responded or retaliated to attacks. This marked the first time that they would go on the offensive. Seeing the tactical advantages of the Solomon Islands to the northeast of Australia, both America and Japan needed control of these key points to have the upper hand in the Pacific. An airfield that was being built on Guadalcanal became the goal of three land invasions and seven fierce naval battles.

August 7, 1942–February 9, 1943

A large force of American soldiers landed on Guadalcanal and took over the airfield on the western part of the island, surprising the outnumbered Japanese that were stationed there. Renamed by the United States as Henderson Field, the ability to use the island to land and fly out aircraft for attacks on nearby countries made this a coveted prize as well as the harbor on Florida Island nearby, that they also regained (Lumen Learning, 2019).

Although the invasion was known as Operation Watchtower, the U.S. Marines jokingly called it "Operation Shoestring" because of the way it was so quickly thrown together without enough maps, planes, and infrastructure. But the element of surprise, force, and some good weather aided the Allies in a quick turnaround of possession of the critical areas (Neikirk, 2022).

The Japanese responded in the early hours of the morning by

hitting the enemy fleet that was stationed close by for support. The quick retaliation was a disaster for the Allies as three American cruisers and one Australian cruiser were put out of action all in the space of half an hour. Over the next few months, the fighting would shift from land skirmishes to intense naval stand-offs, with continuous air support raging in the skies over the islands (Lumen Learning, 2019).

While the United States managed to secure the airfield during the day, the Japanese would counter with night raids attempting to retake the island by sending in more men. At the beginning of November, a massive strike by the Japanese took place with warships providing support from the sea while thousands of troops landed in an attempt to capture Henderson Field, but the Americans successfully defeated them (Lumen Learning, 2019).

In the end, the United States won the battle without knowing it. The Japanese secretly pulled all their men off the island at the end of January 1943, and the Americans only realized later that they were the only ones left on Guadalcanal (Neikirk, 2022). By February 9, the Americans had total control of the island. It was a victory that cost the United States only 1,600 men, while the Japanese lost over 24,000. Both navies suffered as each side lost 24 warships (Lumen Learning, 2019).

Strategically it was a huge blow for Japan after losing at Midway. They no longer had the access and control over southeast Asia that they wanted.

AMAZING FACTS

- *Douglas Munro was the only Coast Guardsman to receive a Medal of Honor when he volunteered to operate a landing craft to ferry troops and was shot in the head in the middle of an ambush by the Japanese (Neikirk, 2022).*

- *Japan attacked the American mainland several times. On June 21, 1942, a Japanese submarine shelled the coastal defenses at Fort Stevens in Oregon. And then on September 9, 1942, they dropped incendiary bombs in the forests of southern Oregon. The forests were unseasonably wet, and the fires failed to spread.*
- *In 1944, the Japanese launched Operation Fu-Go, using "fire balloons" to float 9,300 incendiary bombs across the Pacific Ocean on the wind. Only 350 bombs landed, and most failed to start any fires.*

BATTLE OF EL ALAMEIN

The fighting in North Africa had proven to be tough. The conditions were harsh, and it took many of the Allies a while to adapt against Rommel's well-oiled German divisions. Both sides had already faced off in July at El Alamein, a strategic point that would allow control over Egypt and the Suez Canal. The first battle had ended in a stalemate with neither the Allies nor the Axis forces gaining or losing any ground. The second time they met, however, proved to be the moment that power shifted in Africa.

October 23–November 11

With double the number of tanks and soldiers as the German-Italian force, General Montgomery devised a plan to break the defenses that Rommel had set. While a diversion attack took place in the south, on the evening of October 23, engineers assisted tanks and men to push through the minefields (Gilbert, 2018b). With heavy artillery on the Axis forces, the sky lit up, making way for the infantry to begin their assault. It was slow going, and Rommel held off Montgomery's slow approach that almost cost the Allies as it looked as though the German commander was going to gain ground.

Field Marshal Montgomery

But a shift in plans on November 2, gave the Australian and New Zealand contingent the go-ahead to use their experience to find a way through the heavy minefields. Eventually, a path opened and allowed British tanks to pour across until they met with Rommel's Panzers where a fierce deadlock ensued with heavy losses on both sides.

The fighting raged on until it became clear to Rommel that he could no longer hold the line, and despite Hitler's orders to remain and fight, there was no alternative but to retreat. By November 4, the Germans had already begun withdrawing while the Italians were left to face the oncoming British because they had no transport. Any chance of catching the Germans slipped away as the Allies moved too slowly, but the victory had already been won (Gilbert, 2018b).

The death toll for the Axis came to 9,000 compared to the

Allied count of 4,800 dead (Gilbert, 2018b). The El Alamein victory was a decisive moment in the North African operations in WW2 as it was the first time that the British had won against the Germans. This prompted Winston Churchill to say (History Collection, 2016):

> *"Before Alamein, we never had a victory. After Alamein, we never had a defeat."*

OPERATION TORCH

Instead of attacking Europe head on, the commanders of the Allied forces decided that ending the desert war would not only give them a victory but allow them to open a second front against the Axis Powers. As the first amphibious assault by the Allies, it proved to be the end of the German-Italian occupation of North Africa, and the first combined success.

November 8–16

With Rommel's men fleeing from El Alamein, the timing was perfect to inflict more damage to the enemy along the Mediterranean coast. Under command of Eisenhower, U.S. troops were the first to land in Morocco where they encountered the Vichy French (the puppet French government that supported the Axis Powers). Most surrendered peacefully, but a few units fought the invaders. After two days of sporadic battles in Casablanca, Algiers, and Oran, all French resistance stopped as an armistice was signed on November 10 (Hewitt, n.d.).

As the Vichy French government was no longer active, the Germans raced to occupy the south of France, and seize all its remaining warships.

11

MAJOR EVENTS AND BATTLES— 1943

WARSAW GHETTO UPRISING

The Germans were ruthless in their control of the people, and with the Gestapo and SS watching every move, it was difficult to show any resistance. The consequences of such actions saw many people ending up in concentration camps or being executed. But it did not stop the anger and spirit of the citizens against the brutalities they were seeing. The Warsaw Ghetto Uprising was the first serious defiance by a group in WW2 against German occupation.

April 19–May 16

The Germans had set up a wall on November 15, 1940, to contain over 400,000 Jews, and separate them from the rest of the population. Most were denied the chance to work in normal jobs with forced labor being compulsory for boys and men. Certain religious holidays and rituals were banned, although many secretly continued. The rations of food were under the basic minimum, and almost 90% was obtained through smuggling supplies across the wall (The Holocaust Explained, n.d.-b).

Warsaw Ghetto

At the end of 1942, the Germans began to move thousands out of the ghetto to the Treblinka concentration camp until only 50,000 remained. In January of 1943, people that had lined up to be taken out broke ranks and fought off the German soldiers. Most of those who resisted were killed, but the Jews began preparing for retaliation (The Holocaust Explained, n.d.-b).

On April 19, the Nazis attacked, and were met with immediate resistance from Jews with handmade weapons forcing the Germans to retreat. A systematic destruction of the ghetto followed as the Nazis began to move from one building to the next burning and demolishing until every one of the 42,000 Jews had been rounded up and taken to Treblinka. It took 27 days to crush the uprising, and although it was a defeat for the Jews, it inspired many others who did not agree with the German occupation (The Holocaust Explained, n.d.-b).

BATTLE OF KURSK

Most historians point to D-Day being the moment when the tide turned against the Germans, but the Battle of Kursk marked a crushing defeat from which the Germans never recovered. One of the biggest confrontations of tanks in WW2 was Hitler's last attempt to gain an advantage in Russia.

July 5–August 23

Hitler delayed his attack, giving the Soviets time to prepare. A large salient (a defensive belt that stretches out into enemy territory) was set around the city of Kursk to delay any immediate attack. These were filled with landmines, trenches, barbed wire, and other fortifications.

Armed with 3,000 tanks (including some new and untested ones), the Germans launched Operation Citadel, but their initial offensive was delayed by heavy Soviet fire on July 5. At first, the Wehrmacht made steady but slow progress until they came to a complete standstill in the north. The southern division pushed through, threatening to break the Soviets but met with five tank brigades. The Battle of Prokhorovka involved more than 1,200 tanks with heavy losses on both sides. Again, the Germans could not move any closer to Kursk (SKY History, n.d.).

With problems in Sicily, Hitler had to divert some of his forces to Italy to stop an Allied attack there. This weakened his invasion of Kursk even more. Meanwhile, the Soviets had been holding a large reserve force for just this moment and began to push the

Germans back. The Nazi initiative had been lost, and Hitler's Russian invasion had been crushed, opening the way for the Soviets to begin moving toward Berlin.

AMAZING FACTS

- *Soviet Commander Nikolai Vatutin ordered that his tanks be buried, so that the Germans could only see the top, and be drawn in closer which would eliminate the advantage of long-range guns, and protect the Soviet tanks (Redhead, 2018).*

OPERATION HUSKY

The next step for the Allies after North Africa was to concentrate on Italy, to get a foothold in Europe, but also to eliminate one of the Axis Powers from the war. Despite the clash of personalities in the Allied forces, and bad weather conditions, the operation was successful in pushing the Germans back, and freeing the south of the country.

July 9–August 17

Named Operation Husky, the invasion of Sicily involved 150,000 troops landing on the shores of Sicily (Huxen, 2017). Even though the weather was bad, the Allies pushed through, surprising the Axis forces who were not expecting them to try until the storm had passed.

The Italian forces by this stage were not at full strength, and a day after Mussolini was deposed and arrested on July 24, these troops withdrew. The Germans, however, resisted with strong fighting, but they had lost any advantage, and it was not to their benefit to continue. In August, 100,000 Nazi troops left the island overnight, so Allied troops reached Messina finding no one left to fight them (Huxen, 2017).

Italy as a force had been removed from WW2, and Mussolini was on the run.

AMAZING FACTS

- *In Operation Mincemeat, the body of a homeless person was dressed up with false papers, and left for the Germans to find, and be led to think that attacks were aimed at Sardinia and Corsica. It worked so well that the Nazis were still expecting the attacks even while they were fighting in Sicily (Huxen, 2017).*

ITALIAN CAMPAIGN

Although the United States was against the decision to invade Italy at first, it complied since the British saw it as a major step in securing Europe and dealing a harsh blow to the Axis Powers. With Italy in chaos, it seemed like the right idea at the time, but it proved to be much harder than they thought. The cost of reaching Rome was higher than the Allies had hoped.

September 1943–May 1945

With Mussolini removed from office, an interim government continued to follow Germany's orders although talks of surrender were rumored. The Allies faced a difficult offensive as they battled terrain, weather, and Nazis. The mountains and poor roads slowed the advance of troops into the country, and the Germans were well fortified with machine gun nests, barbed wire, and other defenses.

The Allies moved into Naples on October 1, and later that month, King Emmanuel III declared war on Germany. Even though key cities like Rome were taken in 1944, and other victories along the way, the fighting would continue through to the end of WW2. With Allied forces being withdrawn to take part in the invasion planned at Normandy, it was left to other divisions and Italian partisans to finish the job. It was only completed when Mussolini was executed, and German forces surrendered in Italy on May 1, 1945 (National WW2 Museum, 2022b).

12

MAJOR EVENTS AND BATTLES—1944

BATTLE OF MONTE CASSINO

Part of the Italian Campaign to liberate the country from fascist die-hards and German forces, each battle was more of a skirmish as soldiers had to adapt to the mountains and weather that hampered normal operations. The Allies wanted to reach Rome that signified a victory in their aim to take over Italy, but they had to break through the Gustav Line first that the Germans had set up to stop them.

January 17–May 19

The Germans set up their main force along the line at Monte Cassino by the only road that runs past the historic Monastery that celebrated St. Benedict. There was no other way through because of the winter, but to fight the Nazis who were entrenched there. At first, they were careful not to target the Abbey as it was protected under the Concordat of 1933, but as the Germans were using it to defend their line, they decided to ignore that agreement (The Holocaust Explained, n.d.-a).

The Allies launched their first offensive on January 17 but had to pull back after almost a month of fighting uphill against the Germans. With heavy losses, they had to figure out another way to breach the Nazi defenses. On February 15, the Abbey itself was bombed as the Allies suspected the Germans were using it as a lookout. A total of 250 civilians died in the blasts (The Holocaust Explained, n.d.-a).

The third attack began the following month, in March, after a huge bombing campaign allowed the Allies to move through the town, but they failed to take the Abbey being held by German paratroopers. After more losses, the Allies fell back to regroup for another attempt.

On May 11, Polish divisions managed to breach the German line, and raced to the top of the Monastery where they planted their flag. The Allies had shattered the Gustav Line (Winter Line) and the way was open to march to Rome, which they did a month later. But the price of their success was heavy, with the Allies suffering 55,000 casualties, and the Germans losing 20,000 men (The Holocaust Explained, n.d.-a).

AMAZING FACTS

- *The Monte Cassino Monastery has been damaged and rebuilt before:*
- *In 884, the Saracens burned it down, but it was later rebuilt.*
- *Napoleon's troops sacked it in 1799, and it was restored.*
- *After the Allies bombed it, it was rebuilt and reconsecrated by the Pope in 1964 (Grand Voyage Italy, 2018).*

OPERATION ARGUMENT—"BIG WEEK"

The Allies recognized that the dreaded Luftwaffe would need to be taken out of the picture, or severely damaged in some way, for a successful invasion. Rather than just engage one-on-one, the plan was to slow the production of airplanes, so that Hitler would not have enough to counterattack later. This spelled the end of the Luftwaffe as the superior flying force of WW2.

February 20–February 25

Lt. Gen. James "Jimmy" Doolittle came from his successful run on Japan to take command of Operation Argument. Up until then, the only way to engage with the Germans was through "bait-and-kill" methods where bombers would fly up and lure the Germans in closer for an Allied fighter to come and take it out. But the new fighters were fitted with extra fuel tanks, so they could remain with bombers right up to their destinations and back (Wueschner, 2019).

More than 1,000 bombers accompanied by 600 fighters flew out on February 20 to attack German aircraft factories, and other related industries. At first, the Germans were so surprised to see Americans flying so deep into their country that they failed to react quickly enough to inflict much damage. Every day, a formation of bombers and fighters left for Germany, totaling 6,000 sorties (airplane charges). But by the end of the week, the number of planes downed by the Germans had risen to 357 bombers and 28 fighters. In the end, Leipzig, Stuttgart, and Gotha's industrial areas were all hit hard, bringing the manufacturing of enemy planes to a crawl (Wueschner, 2019).

By the time of the Normandy invasions, the Luftwaffe had to withdraw many of its fighters as they could not compete with the combined forces of the United States and the RAF.

AMAZING FACTS

- *Over 100,000 Allied bomber crewmen were killed over Europe.*

OPERATION OVERLORD—"D-DAY"

By this stage, the Italians had been disarmed as a real threat, and the Germans were being pushed back out of Russia into their own country. For the Allied forces, the main focus in Europe was reclaiming France. Without any harbors or ports under their control, troops would need to land at Normandy, the only accessible beach head. But the Germans were ready for them, and it would need to be one of the biggest combined naval, air, and land operations ever to make it a success.

June 6–August 30

Eisenhower had started working on plans for different scenarios for a final invasion as early as 1941, but Operation Overlord was only adopted in 1943 (Keegan, 2018). Once the politicians had agreed, troops from 12 different countries had begun assembling months before, preparing for the invasion of Nazi-occupied France. These consisted mainly of soldiers from America, Britain, and Canada, but there were divisions that joined from Australia, Belgium, Czechoslovakia, Holland, France, Greece, New Zealand, Norway, Rhodesia, South Africa, and Poland.

AMAZING FACTS

- *To build up resources for the invasion, British factories increased production, and in the first half of 1944, 9 million tons of supplies and equipment crossed from North America to Britain. Over 1.4 million American servicemen arrived during 1943–1944 to take part in the invasion.*

Hitler was aware of the impending invasion, although he was not sure where it would take place. Rommel was given the task of fortifying the coastline, and ended up constructing 2,400 miles of bunkers, minefields with 4 million mines, and other obstacles that came to be known as the "Atlantic Wall" (Keegan, 2018).

To throw the enemy off, the Allies launched Operation Bodyguard to fool the Germans into thinking they would invade Calais, the shortest distance across the Channel from England. False radio transmissions and radar pictures were broadcast of inflatable tanks and dummy landing craft in Kent. These proved successful enough to delay Hitler and Rommel from moving their army to Normandy for seven weeks (Keegan, 2018).

On June 6, paratroopers were sent in ahead to secure key bridges that would be needed once the soldiers landed on the beaches. By the time the landing crafts began to hit the beach and unload their men, the airborne division had successfully captured the bridges. At 6:30 a.m. British and Canadian troops stormed onto Gold, Juno, Utah, and Sword beaches with little resistance. However, the fifth beach of Omaha was where the Germans had stationed their machine gunners, and after more than 2,000 casualties, the Americans finally pushed inland (Keegan, 2018).

Beach Landing

On that first day, 156,000 infantrymen stormed the beaches, three times the number of Germans that were stationed there to hold them off. Without Rommel to oversee events, the German response was slightly delayed, but after some time, Hitler ordered Panzer units to drive through to Sword and Juno beaches that would have completely crippled the landings. But they were met with stiff resistance from anti-tank gunners who held them off (Roos, 2019).

Over the next few days, a total of 2.5 million men were ferried onto the beaches along with 500,000 vehicles and a mass of supplies. Although the Germans were putting up fierce resistance, they were running out of reinforcements, and had very few Luftwaffe to assist in the air. On top of that, they were running out of officers, some of whom died, while others were dismissed for admitting defeat (Roos, 2019).

AMAZING FACTS

- *There were no harbors that could be used on the Normandy coast, so two ready-built harbors were taken in sections across the English Channel and assembled off Omaha Beach and Gold Beach. The Mulberry harbors were to be used until major French ports could be captured and brought back into use after repair. Parts of these harbors can still be seen off the Normandy beaches today.*

Normandy Supply

At the end of June, the Port of Cherbourg was taken back from the Germans, a tactical victory that opened the way for ships and supplies to be brought in. Up until that time, ready-built harbors had been designed with floating piers, but the weather caused these to be less effective than beach landings using different vessels.

July 25 saw the Americans break through a gap in the German's tank line, and despite Hitler's attempts to squash it, they advanced. By that stage, the Nazi strongholds were being overrun, and the order was given for the Germans to withdraw. Even though the bridges had been destroyed, they still managed to cross the Seine to safety with the Allies moving up behind them.

As the enemy raced across the border, resistance forces revolted against the Germans in Paris. Eisenhower changed direction, and instead of bypassing, he reinforced the fighting on August 24. The following morning, the Nazi commander of the city surrendered. Operation Overlord had reached all its objectives, but with 300,000 German soldiers, and 200,000 Allied soldiers perishing as a result (Keegan, 2018).

AMAZING FACTS

- *A practice run for D-Day was staged two months before along an English beach. It was called "Exercise Tiger," and the Germans found out about it, and torpedoed American tank landing ships killing 749 soldiers. It was said to be worse than the actual D-Day on Omaha Beach (Roos, 2019)!*
- *The "D" in D-Day stands simply for "day" and was used to describe the first day of any large military operation.*

OPERATION BAGRATION

The Germans now faced war on both sides. As the Allied nations landed at Normandy, forcing Hitler's men back toward the Seine River, Stalin's Red Army was leading its own offensive to push the Nazis out of Russia, all the way to Germany. The Operation was far bigger in scale than D-Day, cost more lives, and was much more effective. It also allowed the communists to rush into regions that they had had their eye on for so long.

June 22–August 19

Bagration, named after a famous Russian general, was part of Stalin's promise when the Big Three met at Tehran to launch an offensive that would support what the Allies were doing in France. Once again, the Germans fell for deception as the Soviets threw them false information that the attack would come from Ukraine. Army Group Center (as the German force was known) sent reserves down to that area, leaving themselves open to a much larger Red Army that took them by surprise (Mansoor, 2019).

With 1.2 million Soviet troops, 5,000 tanks, and 6,000 aircraft, the Germans were outmatched seven to one in every department resulting in a quarter of its military strength being lost in the space of 10 days. Of the 34 divisions of the Army Group Center, only six remained once the Soviets had cleared their way through. Hitler's command to stand and fight spelled only certain death in the face of an oncoming wave. The speed and force at which the Red Army swept through left scores of prisoners behind, and 12 million Germans and East Prussians heading west to avoid the Red Army, creating a major refugee problem for the German government (Mansoor, 2019).

Stalin's forces opened the rest of the Soviet Union as they reached Poland. They were now in the prime position to march into Germany, and finally Berlin itself. Stalin wanted to be sure that he did not miss out on what was to be gained from taking the Nazi capital city.

In the two months of fierce fighting, the Germans lost 400,000 while 180,000 of the Red Army's soldiers were killed (Mansoor, 2019).

AMAZING FACTS

- *On July 20, 1944, Claus von Stauffenberg attempted to assassinate Hitler, inside his Wolf's Lair field headquarters. Hitler survived when a bomb planted in a briefcase exploded but failed to kill him after one of his generals moved the case to get a better look at a map.*

OPERATION MARKET GARDEN

With the Germans having retreated behind the natural borders of rivers, it was vital to try and find routes that the Allies could use to chase them. The only way to do this would be over bridges! By making sure that these crossings were not destroyed, the Germans could be pursued, and the war would have been over quickly. But the plan hit problems and ultimately failed.

September 17–September 27

Field Marshal Montgomery persuaded Eisenhower to go along with his ambitious plan of a two-part strike on specific bridges in the Netherlands crossing the Meuse, Waal, and Rhine Rivers. The Market part would see 40,000 airborne soldiers land at three specific points to locate and fight off any enemy presence at the bridges. The Garden portion was the ground forces that would come and secure those crossings (Bluhm, 2022).

The troops that were flown in and dropped at Nijmegen took a few bridges as did those that landed by Eindhoven. Arnhem proved too difficult to reach when the division landed six miles away and ended up having to fight their way to get even close to the bridge.

But when the ground force tried to get to either Eindhoven or Nijmegen, they met with heavy German resistance that was too quick, and with Luftwaffe support, they turned the tables by blowing up several bridges rather than let the Allies have them (Bluhm, 2022).

Those at Arnhem had fought their way closer but could not make it, and they ended up being surrounded. Rescuing this troop signaled the end of a disastrous operation. Around 15,000 Allies were killed or wounded, while 6,000 were taken prisoner (Bluhm, 2022).

BATTLE OF THE BULGE

A last-ditch attempt to split the Allied forces took place in the Ardennes Forest of Belgium. In Germany's final offensive campaign on the western front of WW2, Hitler once again relied on speed and force to push the Allies like a wedge ("bulge") and divide them.

December 16–January 25, 1945

The mist over the Ardennes, the crisscross of rivers and valleys, and the freezing conditions were an advantage for the Germans at first. It limited any air support for the Americans and forced the troops into chaos as the Panzer divisions rushed in toward the Meuse River. The U.S. soldiers were caught by surprise, and it looked as though Hitler's gamble was going to work.

At least 1,000 German tanks and 200,000 men raced ahead with little time to even take prisoners, ending in massacres of U.S. soldiers and civilians at Stavelot and Malmedy. Seizing important crossroads, it looked as though the promise of an Allied victory was not going to be seen (U.S. Army, 2000).

But things changed as General Patton swung his Third U.S. Army around so quickly that it stunned the enemy exposing their flank. But it was not just the might of a large force that proved the downfall of the Nazi offensive. Small groups of engineers and paratroopers valiantly fought off and destroyed bridges forcing the Panzers into a bottleneck where they ran out of fuel (U.S. Army, 2000).

With Patton's men attacking from the south, and the First U.S. Army countering from the north, the Germans were suddenly on the back foot looking for an escape route. Not only were they on the run again, but the Germans had lost too many men and precious tanks along the way. The road was now open for the Allies to chase them into their own country.

AMAZING FACTS

- *Hitler's generals advised him not to go ahead with the Ardennes Offensive as they realized there were problems with the strategy, but once again the Führer ignored their protests (Andrews, 2018).*
- *The Germans used stolen U.S. uniforms to sneak behind enemy lines to cut communication wires, change road signs, and sabotage bridges until roadblocks were set up with typical American questions to catch the culprits (Andrews, 2018).*

Germans Changing Signs

13

HOW THE WAR ENDED

BATTLE OF IWO JIMA

Officially, Iwo Jima was part of Japan, and a U.S. attack would be the first time they were invading their homeland. At 750 miles away from the capital of Japan, it was a strategic point to launch bomber aircraft strikes from, and a crucial political gain if the Americans could take the island.

February 19–March 25

The struggle to capture Iwo Jima came down to the Japanese commander, Lt. Gen. Kuribayashi's decision to drag the battle out with as much injury and death as his army could inflict on the U.S. troops (Hudson, 2018). With an entire network of tunnels running underground, hundreds of protected sites for guns, and other booby traps that were hidden around the island, it was designed to be a tough task for the Americans to liberate it.

Thinking it would be over in a week, the United States took key sites like the airfields and Mount Suribachi early on. But they found themselves still on the island 36 days after the first landing, facing fierce resistance from Kuribayashi's men who had been given orders not to surrender. With hills that had nicknames like "The Meat Grinder," the battles turned out to be grim and bloody with a high number of casualties (Hudson, 2018).

AMAZING FACTS

- *The raising of the flag on Mount Suribachi was photographed by Joe Rosenthal, and quickly became an iconic symbol for the Marine Corps, dedicated to all those who gave their lives in military service to the United States (Hudson, 2018).*

Iwo Jima Statue

BATTLE OF OKINAWA

It was another island littered with caves and places to hide which the United States knew was going to be a battle just like Iwo Jima.

Although the Americans had the upper hand in numbers and firepower, the fierce resistance made progress slow. But it was the Japanese response in committing suicide that pushed the death toll way up.

April 1–June 22

With 180,000 U.S. troops, backed by 12,000 aircraft, and 1,600 ships, the initial landing was met with little opposition, and 50,000 troops were able to move across half the island within the next three days. The reply from the Japanese came at sea, targeting the Allied fleet that was positioned off the coast. More than 350 kamikaze planes thundered down onto the ships as well as manned missiles which took out 26 American Naval vessels (Ray, 2020a). These suicidal attacks were costly but effective, and the United States had to change strategies to combat them.

Back on land, even with additional men joining in, the invasion had stalled as troops encountered caves with hundreds of booby-trapped entrances, and tunnels from which the Japanese launched scathing attacks. Attempts were made to bomb the main hill where the enemy was hiding, but it had little effect. The Japanese had to be rooted out bit by bit, and only on May 16, was this feature finally taken.

Okinawa Fighting

The fighting moved into the suburbs with intense house-to-house combat against the Japanese troops. Civilians had been told that surrendering was not an option, and over 100,000 men, women, and children killed themselves rather than be taken prisoner. The result of Okinawa was a bloody battle with an extremely high number of casualties ranging from 12,000 U.S. soldiers killed to 110,000 Japanese soldiers that died (Ray, 2020a).

FALL OF BERLIN

Even though it was clear that the Germans were backed into a corner, they did not surrender. With the full might of the Soviets on their doorstep, they put up their last fight to maintain the capital city. But they were outnumbered and ran out of supplies until even Hitler eventually saw no way out and committed suicide.

April 16–May 2

While 2.5 million Red Army soldiers surrounded Berlin, ready for revenge on what the Wehrmacht had inflicted on their people in Operation Barbarossa, 1 million German soldiers barricaded themselves, ready for the fight (Robinson, 2020). After a massive bombardment from artillery guns, the tanks moved in, but they were restricted from moving by the rubble from all the explosions. So, it came down to hand-to-hand combat that moved house to house and street by street.

Rather than surrender to the Russians, because they knew that they would only receive brutal torture or death, the Nazis chose to fight, many of them with no fear of dying for their country. Although they fought bravely, they could not hold off the power of the Soviet response.

Hitler continued to give out orders from his bunker even though he did not have enough men or ammunition, and Stalin was fixated on capturing the Reichstag, a symbol of all the Nazis had stood for.

The intense fighting lasted 17 days leaving 200,000 dead. By April 30, Hitler had finally admitted defeat by shooting himself in the head which gave the Garrison Commander the chance to surrender (Robinson, 2020). Five days later, General Jodl of the German army signed the unconditional surrender of Nazi Germany. The war in Europe was over.

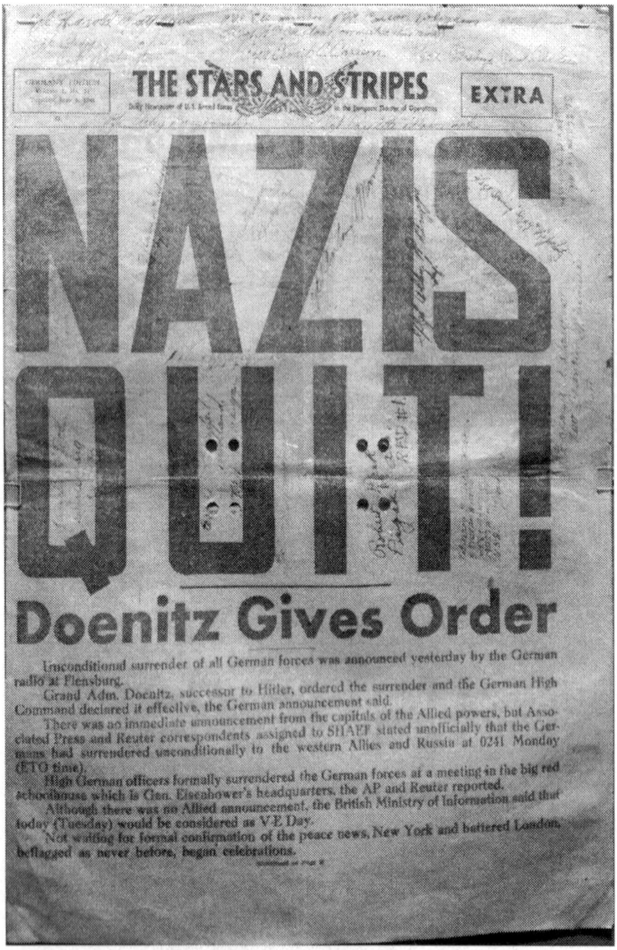

THE STARS AND STRIPES

EXTRA

NAZIS QUIT!

Doenitz Gives Order

Unconditional surrender of all German forces was announced yesterday by the German radio at Flensburg.

Grand Adm. Doenitz, successor to Hitler, ordered the surrender and the German High Command declared it effective, the German announcement said.

There was no immediate announcement from the capitals of the Allied powers, but Associated Press and Reuter correspondents assigned to SHAEF stated unofficially that the Germans had surrendered unconditionally to the western Allies and Russia at 0241 Monday (ETO time).

High German officers formally surrendered the German forces at a meeting in the big red schoolhouse which is Gen. Eisenhower's headquarters, the AP and Reuter reported.

Although there was no Allied announcement, the British Ministry of Information said that today (Tuesday) would be considered as V-E Day.

Not waiting for formal confirmation of the peace news, New York and battered London, beflagged as never before, began celebrations.

Germany Surrenders Headline

AMAZING FACTS

- *The Soviet 203mm Howitzer B-4 was an artillery gun that the Germans called "Stalin's sledgehammer" because it knocked out pillboxes and could bring a multi-story building down in under an hour. But it met its match when it failed to knock down the "Zoo flak tower" (fortified towers built to protect Berlin from*

Allied bomber raids) after hitting it again and again, it only managed to damage one corner (Egorov, 2020).

THE ATOMIC BOMBINGS

Even though it was clear that the Japanese were being pushed back and were losing the war, they vowed to continue fighting. Fearing an invasion could lead to 1 million U.S. soldiers being killed, the risk was considered too high. It was an extreme move, and many historians disagree with the magnitude of what happened next, but the dice were rolled, and it fell on making a bold move rather than a drawn-out battle. Truman, the new U.S. President, finally authorized the use of atomic weapons that brought the war to an abrupt standstill.

August 6 and 9

After testing in the New Mexico desert, U.S. bombers set out for a surprise attack on August 6, where the first atomic bomb, named "Little Boy," was dropped over the city of Hiroshima. Within minutes, half the city had disappeared. The massive blast generated a shock wave and winds that flattened homes even further out. Most of the 140,000 people died because of the flash burns and intense heat that measured several million degrees Celsius, and the later effects of radiation (Kimball, n.d.).

Atomic Bomb

Even after this, there was no word from the Japanese government!

Three days later, "Fat Man," the second atomic bomb was flown out and dropped on Nagasaki with the same crippling effects, killing 74,000 people from the first blast to the radioactive illnesses that claimed lives later (Kimball, n.d.).

Emperor Hirohito announced the surrender of Japan and signed a formal declaration in front of General MacArthur aboard the USS *Missouri* on September 2 (D-Day, n.d.). What became known as V-J day (Victory over Japan) also signaled the end of WW2.

AMAZING FACTS

- *Operation Meetinghouse was a bomb attack that was more destructive than the atomic bombs. It was a napalm attack on March 9, 1945, that killed 100,000 people in Tokyo with many more injured (Atkins, 2018).*
- *"Hiroshima Shadows" were outlines or shadows of people and objects that were burned into the ground because of the intensity of the blast of the atomic bomb dropped on that city (Atkins, 2018).*
- *The Oleander became the official flower of Hiroshima when it was the first one to blossom there after the atomic attack (Atkins, 2018).*

14

HEROIC FEATS

Intense situations often bring out the most courageous acts in people where they rise above what they're facing to achieve the unthinkable. These are heroes! Often because of the nature of war, these are soldiers that perform incredible acts of bravery, but there are many, in other fields, that also stand up to go beyond their normal call of duty. WW2 is filled with hundreds of these moments—too many to relate. Here are just a few of the outstanding heroes.

MILITARY

Audie Murphy

Murphy grew up as a Texas farm boy. His father left the family when he was young, and after his mother died when he was 16, he watched as his 11 brothers and sisters were sent to orphanages or other families (Arlington National Cemetery, 2019). Looking for a way out, he lied about his age and enlisted in the army.

Including the Medal of Honor, he received every military award for valor available from the United States Army, as well as French and Belgian awards for heroism.

But his most notable act came on January 26, 1945, when he jumped onto a burning tank and held back the enemy with a machine gun for almost an hour, killing 50 Germans (Arlington National Cemetery, 2019). After returning home as a hero, he became an actor in a few movies because of his good looks.

Hershel Woodrow "Woody" Williams

During the battle of Iwo Jima, Woody saw that tanks were making slow progress, and as a Demolitions Sergeant, he took it upon himself to open the way. On February 23, 1945, he charged forward in the face of machine-gun fire to prepare demolition charges. Over a period of four hours, he went back and forth grabbing equipment and engaging with the enemy.

At one point, he jumped onto a pillbox where Japanese soldiers were firing at the enemy and pushed his flamethrower into the vent killing the occupants (CMHS, 2022). When he was later cornered by the enemy, he single-handedly operated six flamethrowers against Japanese forces, keeping them at bay for several hours, all at the age of 21.

It was men like Woody that went the extra mile, and helped his unit to move forward, and conquer the enemy. He was awarded the Medal of Honor for his unselfish act of bravery.

Desmond Doss

Doss refused to carry a weapon because he did not believe in taking lives, but that did not stop him from engaging in the Battle of Okinawa. Instead of fighting, he was made a medic, but he was not popular because of his belief not to hold or fire a gun.

But all that changed, when he worked tirelessly for 12 hours in the face of enemy fire to treat the wounded, and drag them to the edge of Hacksaw Ridge, and lower them down (Kelly, 2017). When he was later wounded in the legs by shrapnel and shot by a sniper, he was always looking to see where others needed his help, and even gave up his stretcher for another soldier.

He saved 75 lives during his time at Okinawa and was awarded the Medal of Honor by President Truman who said that it was a "greater honor than being president" (Kelly, 2017).

Matthew Urban

Captain Urban was stubborn, refusing to be evacuated many times when he was repeatedly wounded in battle. He saw the importance of leadership, and despite his injuries, bravely led his unit to overcome the enemy. At one stage, he stood in front of the Germans with a bazooka to fend them off while they fired at him.

When he heard his division was struggling in France, he left the hospital and limped back into battle to jump on a tank while being shot at to encourage his men forward in battle.

Even when he was shot in the neck on September 3, 1944, he refused to leave until he was sure that the soldiers in his unit had overcome the enemy and gained the Meuse River crossing (Sterner, 2022).

For his incredible leadership under fire, he received numerous awards including seven Purple Hearts as well as the Medal of Honor many years later after the war had ended (Sterner, 2022).

Richard Bong

The greatest U.S. fighter ace of WW2, Bong destroyed 40 enemy planes during his time in the war (AFHSD, n.d.). He received 25 medals for his incredible feats plus the Medal of Honor.

In September 1944, he had fulfilled his training and time in combat and was not required to assist, but he volunteered in 30 missions in which he shot down 12 planes over Borneo and the Philippines (AFHSD, n.d.). He died when his plane failed during a routine exercise back in the States.

With over 200 missions and 500 hours of combat time, he became the top ace in the U.S. Air Force—a hero of the skies.¶

Ruby Bradley

The Angel in Fatigues was Ruby Bradley, a U.S. Army Nurse. She was already enlisted in the army when Pearl Harbor was bombed, stationed in Luzon in the Philippines. She was captured and spent the rest of the war as a POW in Japanese camps.

Despite the horrific conditions, she continued to care for starving children by giving them her food, even though rations were two half cups of rice a day. She performed surgeries and delivered babies, often without the necessary equipment which amazed even the Japanese. After three years in captivity, she was freed by U.S. troops and went home to the United States, but she was back in Asia, serving as a nurse in the Korean War. She received over 30 different medals of honor.

Charles Joseph Coward

Coward escaped seven times from German prisons during WW2, ultimately being sent to Auschwitz labor camp. One night, he smuggled himself in and out of the camp and reported back to the British about what he'd seen. He became a witness during the Nuremberg and IG Farben Trials (Pitogo, 2013). Not only was he a master of escape, but he helped about 400 Jewish captives to also get out of the camps.

Bhanbhagta Gurung

The Victoria Cross was handed to Gurung, a Gurkha rifleman who stood up to expose his position, so that he could take out a sniper 75 meters away (Tracesofwar, n.d.). Five times, while his unit was pinned down, he rushed into enemy fire to disengage the threat by whatever means he had available, even hand-to-hand combat.

He opened the way for his entire division to press forward and drive back the enemy.

Lachhiman Gurung

Also, a Gurkha Rifleman, his unit was pinned down by the enemy as they threw hand grenades into their trench. Gurung threw two back but the third exploded in his hand. Without his fingers on the right hand, he reloaded and fired with his left, keeping the enemy back by himself. At least 31 soldiers were killed by Gurung, alone, in the four hours he waited out each wave of attack (Tracesofwar, n.d.).

Jack Churchill

Known as "Fighting" Jack Churchill and "Mad Jack," this British trooper was known for his eccentricity in the war. He fought armed only with a longbow, arrows, and a Scottish broadsword. His motto was "any officer who goes into action without his sword is improperly armed" (Bibby, n.d.). Churchill gained notoriety for charging into battle playing the bagpipes. Even after a stint at the Sachsenhausen concentration camp (from which he escaped), he continued his military escapades, walking 93 miles to rejoin the army in Italy.

SPIES AND RESISTANCE FIGHTERS

Virginia Hall: Allied Spy

Known as the "Limping Lady," Hall was one of the most hunted spies by the Third Reich. Working undercover in France, she organized routes, supplies, and information through an extensive spy network that she helped to set up. By 1943, her British organizers realized that it was too dangerous for her to continue, and they pulled her out (Fausone, 2018).

But the Americans saw her as an asset, and sent her back where she continued her work, even encouraging a group of partisans called the Marquis to resist the Nazis by supplying them with weapons (Fausone, 2018).

She was awarded the Distinguished Service Cross, and later went to work for the CIA.

Nancy Wake: Guerrilla Fighter

Nicknamed "The White Mouse," she worked with Marquis groups, even taking command of the rough men at times (Tracesofwar, n.d.). At one stage, she traveled hundreds of kilometers on her own to make radio contact when their communication lines were down. Her ability to organize and get the job done earned her the respect of all those around her, shooting Nazis or blowing up buildings. She once killed an SS sentry with her bare hands.

She was awarded numerous awards from America, Britain, and France.

Noor Inayat Khan: British Spy

Khan was hunted by the Gestapo as they knew about her and what she had been doing, but not who she was. As an operative in France, she remained, despite the arrests of those around her, as she saw the work as too important. She was the lone radio operator for four months in Paris until she was betrayed by a double agent and handed over to the Gestapo who tried in vain to get information from her. She was sent to Berlin, but even there, she remained loyal to the cause. On September 12, 1944, she was shot (Tracesofwar, n.d.).

Eileen Nearne: British Spy

In France in 1944, Nearne worked with a network called "The Wizard" that wired over 100 secret messages back to England (LMC, 2019). To avoid being caught, she moved often and was always very careful, but the German secret police found her in a raid. She managed to destroy all the evidence, but she suffered incredible torture as the Nazis suspected her of espionage.

She never gave in, sticking to her story that she was a French secretary. Sent to many concentration camps, she managed to escape and hide in a church in Leipzig until the Allies freed the country. Nearne died in 2010, and her wartime exploits were only revealed after a search of her apartment uncovered her war medals. She was then given a hero's funeral.

HUMANITARIANS

Irena Sendler

Irena Sendlerowa was a Polish social worker who took on the role of a nurse, so she could save over 2,500 Jewish babies and children by helping them escape and changing their identities once they were out of the Warsaw ghetto (Sedgwick, 2019). By hiding them in ambulances, smuggling them through sewer pipes, or even carrying them out in suitcases, she saved many lives.

Raoul Wallenberg

A Swedish businessman, Wallenberg was made a diplomat, so he could travel to Hungary, and assist in helping Jews escape the horrors that the Nazis had waiting for them in concentration camps. He managed to organize the widest-reaching operation that smuggled Jews out of the country, amounting to nearly 100,000 successful rescues (Pitogo, 2013).

Reports of his disappearance and death show that he may have been arrested shortly before the end of the war and was either killed or died in prison.

Oskar Schindler

Made famous by the movie, *Schindler's List,* he was a German spy, and a Nazi party member, yet he ended up saving the lives of 1,200 Jews (Pitogo, 2013). As a businessman, he owned a factory, and ensured that all the Jews that were employed there were kept safe through his contacts and financial contributions to Hitler's cause.

Chiune Sugihara

As a Japanese diplomat in Lithuania, he issued visas to Jews that he wrote by hand, saving over 6,000 lives (Pitogo, 2013). Rumors mention he even threw visas out the train as he traveled for Jews to collect and use to escape the country. He was given express orders from Japan not to do so, but he did anyway and was dismissed from his post after the war ended.

Henryk Sławik

Sławik was a Polish politician who used his status and role in the community to save 30,000 refugees (Pitogo, 2013). Almost a fifth of these were Jews whom he had given false passports declaring they were Catholics, so they could escape to freedom. His deeds were discovered, and he was executed.

SCIENTISTS

Alan Turing

One of the scientists that paved the way for the modern computer, the world has a lot to thank Turing for. But it was his work overseeing a small group of cryptanalysts during WW2 that he's also known for. Devising a machine that could break the Enigma code that the Germans used, allowed the British to have access to up to 84,000 messages intended for the Nazis every month (Copeland, 2019). It was this breakthrough that gave the Allies the upper hand, being able to know Hitler's plans beforehand. It's thought his work helped to shorten the war by 2–3 years, saving thousands if not millions of lives.

Joan Clarke

Part of the group that cracked the Enigma code, Clarke's brilliance in mathematics gave her a unique advantage in seeing patterns and formulas. This insight gave her the unique ability to be a cryptanalyst, and she worked closely with Alan Turing. She continued to work for the government as a code breaker long after the war.

Jane Hughes Fawcett

Another code breaker, Fawcett was credited for sinking the German battleship *Bismarck* (SMH, 2016). On May 25, 1941, she caught the message of where the Nazi's newest warship was headed, giving the Allies the directions to attack. The next day they tracked the elusive *Bismarck and* sank her.

Jane and Joan (above) are just two of the women of Bletchley Park, where over 8,000 worked including many cryptanalysts. Few received any credit for their work, and many never revealed their work during the war, even later in life.

15

PRISONERS OF WAR

International law is clear that any prisoner of war has certain rights and access to medical and humane treatment regardless of their nationality. But in WW2, these guidelines were often ignored, especially in German and Japanese camps where POWs were given hardly any food, tortured, and exposed to the point of death. The horrific conditions that they endured were some of the worst atrocities during the war.

THE THIRD GENEVA CONVENTION, 1929

The main aim of these conferences held in Geneva, Switzerland was to agree on handling civilians, prisoners of war (POWs), and soldiers who were captured, or not able to fight. Here are some of the main conditions that were to be followed when a person was taken prisoner:

- They must be treated humanely with no acts of violence against them.
- Women must be treated with consideration.
- Only the name, rank, or regiment number needs to be given. No other information can be forced out of the prisoner.
- Prisoners must be kept in places that are hygienic with adequate bedding, warmth, and light.
- Food and water must follow the same rations as a normal depot troop.
- Medical treatment must be available.
- Only those who are able can be made to work, and suitable to their ability to carry out the tasks (ICRC, n.d.).

A total of 54 countries signed the 1929 Convention including Germany, Italy, Britain, and the United States. Japan and Russia, however, did not. Even though these regulations were in place, it did not stop the harsh treatment and terrible living conditions that POWs had to face often ending in death.

GERMANY

For the most part, when it came to the Allies, Germany stuck to the Geneva Convention terms, treating the prisoners as well as could be expected under the conditions. Only the name, rank, and serial number were required when POWs gave their details, but officers did their best to try and trick extra information out of them.

German POW camps were called *Stalags* (short for *Stammlager*) and were situated throughout Nazi-occupied countries (HistoryontheNet, 2018). Once prisoners arrived by train, they would receive two meals of thin soup and bread each day, although this became much less as German supplies ran out.

Red Cross parcels were allowed with *luxury* items of chocolate, biscuits, and other things. Men were housed in wooden barracks stacked with bunk beds and a central coal stove. Some worked, but the biggest drawbacks were hunger and boredom.

The Russians did not enjoy the same treatment. They were given below the daily ration of food or were force-starved, while others suffered from the poor conditions and lack of provisions given to them, resulting in 5,000 deaths a day (USHMM, 2019). This number increased when winter set in.

Instead of giving medical treatment, the Nazis solved the problem by removing the wounded Russians and shooting them. Over 65,000 were starved in the Gross-Rosen camp, others were burned alive in Flossenburg, while in Majdanek and Mauthausen countless were shot (USHMM, 2019). By the beginning of 1942, 2 million Soviet POWs had died.

AMAZING FACTS

- *A British soldier escaped to see his German girlfriend and came back to the camp he was at over 200 times without guards ever knowing (Kickassfacts, 2015).*

JAPAN

Japan's harsh treatment of its prisoners was a sore point long after the war had ended. In total, about 140,000 Allied prisoners were captured, held in camps, and forced to work in coal mines, shipyards, and factories (Hays, 2016). Disease and starvation were a constant threat in these camps, and thousands died as a result. Slave labor of up to 12 hours a day and a deficient diet contributed to a staggering death rate in these camps spread across China, Burma, Korea, and other Asian countries.

The Bataan Death March forced around 80,000 POWs to walk 60 miles to the nearest camp (Hays, 2016). Many died on the way. Others faced indescribable torture and even had to suffer as medical experiments and target practice. One prisoner's body parts were cut off while he was alive, so his captors could see the effects!

The death rate was 27% compared to the low figure of around 4% in German and Italian camps (Hays, 2016). One of the reasons may have been because the Japanese saw surrender as one of the most dishonorable acts preferring to commit suicide rather than be taken captive. They saw it as their job to make these *weak* soldiers suffer for their shame.

AMAZING FACTS

- *Desperate for food, James "Ringer" Edwards, a POW in a Japanese camp, killed a cow to feed his fellow prisoners, but he was caught, and his punishment was to be crucified on a tree using barbed wire for 63 hours. Ringer survived (SOFREP Media Group, 2022)!*

RUSSIA

Stalin always thought that Russia would need 4 million POWs for forced labor to rebuild cities that had been destroyed (Manaev, 2021). Most of these were German soldiers, but the rest were citizens of captured countries made to reconstruct dams, railroads, factories, and other structures.

Conditions in the 240 different camps were not good. As a German POW said, "At first, we had to load two train cars with wood during one work shift, then the norm was increased to three cars. We were forced to work 16 hours a day, on Sundays and holidays, also. We returned to the camp at nine or ten o'clock in the evening, but often at midnight. We received watery soup, and fell asleep, so the next day at five in the morning we would go to work again" (Manaev, 2021).

Food was the biggest issue for prisoners as rations were often below the required quota, and starvation caused many deaths, most of them in the winter. Some historians claim that up to 580,000 died while in prison camps, most of them Germans, while almost 2 million Soviets died in Nazi concentration camps (Manaev, 2021).

AMAZING FACTS

- *Repatriation is the moving back of prisoners to their own country and making sure that they are adequately taken care of. Because there were so many German POWs (2 million), it took almost five years until the last had been properly sent back (Manaev, 2021).*

AMERICA

More than 400,000 Axis prisoners were kept in the United States where camps were set up in rural areas (Garcia, 2009). Many were sent to farms or factories as there was such a shortage of workers at that time.

Life in the camps was sometimes better than their home life, and they received food, facilities, and treatment that was so good, one prisoner described it as a "golden cage" (Garcia, 2009). They could buy certain luxuries with the money they earned. There were hardly any escapes, and most POWs were happy to help America in the war cause.

AMAZING FACTS

- *American girls fell in love with many POWs kept in the United States, especially the Italians, but they were not allowed to marry them. After the war, they were given legal documents to get married in Italy, then come back with their husbands to America (MHN, 2018).*

BRITAIN

During the war, over 400,000 POWs from Italy, Germany, and Ukraine were kept in camps in Britain (Franklin, 2017). There were hardly any escapes as most were content with the treatment they received while being held prisoner. They received the same rations as the ground troops and were paid for work they did.

Others were given the chance to work outside the confines, attending the local churches, joining football leagues, and becoming as much a part of the community as possible (Franklin, 2017).

AMAZING FACTS

- *Pilates was invented by a German POW, Joseph Pilates, held in Knockaloe camp where he developed a system of exercises without using equipment (Historic England, 2018).*
- *Some German officers were kept in luxury rather than a camp, so they would let down their guard while their conversations were monitored allowing the British to learn about the Holocaust, Hitler, and V2 rockets (Kickassfacts, 2015).*
- *Of German POWs, 24,000 settled in Britain after the war. The most famous was Bert Trautman who became famous as a goalkeeper for Manchester City in 1949 and went on to play for 15 years.*

FAMOUS POW'S PRISON ESCAPES

Where there's a prison, there will always be an escape, or somebody trying to get out! In WW2, there are plenty of stories of failed attempts, and those that were so daring and cunning that they succeeded.

The Wooden Horse

Oliver Philpot was part of a group of four men that used a wooden vaulting horse to escape from Stalag Luft III in 1943 (IWM, 2022a). The wooden horse was for the men to exercise, but Philpot and his men used the hollow of it to dig an elaborate tunnel from the middle of the grounds to the outside of the fence. Every day they covered the hole, and scattered the extra sand as they walked, so guards would not notice what they were doing.

Collecting fake identity papers and a compass, Philpot escaped with his group on October 29 (IWM, 2022a). He made it all the way to Sweden.

The Great Escape

Also from Stalag Luft III, Jimmy James and a group of men began digging three tunnels for 200 men to escape (IWM, 2022a). One of the tunnels was discovered, but the men continued with the others until March 25, 1944, when 80 men crawled through (IWM, 2022a). Most were recaptured.

Eichstatt Tunnel

Mike Scott and 65 others escaped in June 1943 using a tunnel from the toilets up a hill to a village chicken coop (IWM, 2022a). Over 50,000 police and guards were dispatched to find the missing men. After two weeks, most of the men were recaptured and sent to Colditz, a notorious castle prison.

16

THE HOLOCAUST

One of the worst events in history, the Holocaust was Nazi Germany's deliberate murder of 6 million Jews including 1 million children, and at least 5 million POWs, Romanians, homosexuals, disabled people, and others that Hitler hated. The hatred he encouraged against the Jews and his devious plan to get rid of them moved him from just another dictator to someone who began a war to a cold-blooded murderer and genocidal maniac.

WHY DID THE NAZIS PERSECUTE THE JEWS?

Whether they just needed a scapegoat or were truly racist, anti-Semitism became one of the main pillars of the Nazi ideology. Much of what they did was centered around getting rid of the Jews —creating land for pure Aryans meant there was no room for anyone else.

It was not a secret. Hitler spelled it out shortly after WWI, in his book *Mein Kampf,* when he said, "Its final objective must unswervingly be the removal of the Jews altogether" (Berenbaum,

2018). He blamed them for everything; the loss of the First World War, the problems in the country, and the fact that they were rich while normal Germans starved. He painted them as people who were greedy for world domination that needed to be stopped.

Racial supremacy was what motivated Hitler and the Nazis. It was not a new idea since anti-Semitism had been around long before as well as nations that wanted to exterminate other races, so they would be the only ones standing in the end. But the Nazis did reinvent it in a chilling new format—they turned it into mass extermination.

KRISTALLNACHT

Jews had been receiving harsh treatment since Hitler began his speeches to the public, drawing attention to their supposed role in Germany's defeat in WWI. In 1933, when Hitler came into power, many Jews lost their jobs in civil service, and a number were ousted from their political roles. Schools instituted quota systems barring too many Jews from attending these institutions, and any books by Jews or Communists were burned.

On November 9, 1938, a well-planned series of attacks took place. Riots exploded and 7,500 Jewish businesses, and 1,000 synagogues were destroyed in acts of vandalism with hundreds of their windows smashed in the process, giving this event the name "Crystal Night" (Berenbaum, 2018). Men were rounded up and arrested, then sent off to newly built concentration camps. It was not the first time the Jews had been targeted in acts of sabotage, but it was the first coordinated violent attack. The police and firemen did nothing except make sure that other businesses were not harmed in the process.

The Jews were blamed for the uprising, and as a people, were fined 1 billion Reichsmarks by Herman Goring (Berenbaum, 2018).

From that moment, Jews found they were not allowed in certain places and schools, and had their properties and goods seized. Any freedom they had enjoyed up until that moment had vanished.

The practice of Jews having to wear a yellow Star of David badge to show who they were came into effect in 1939. Three years later, almost every German-controlled European country had implemented the same protocol. Jews everywhere were being pinpointed, then alienated, and then sent away.

GHETTOS

One of the problems the Nazis had was that they forced Jews out into neighboring countries, but then just as quickly, took over those nations. Over 2 million Jews were added to the problem when Hitler invaded Poland (Berenbaum, 2018). Part of the answer to this was to isolate these unwanted citizens by building ghettos —smaller contained suburbs within the cities. At least 30% of Poland's population was forced into 400 of these urban enclaves (Berenbaum, 2018).

Forced labor was required from those able to handle the long hours and grueling workloads. Restrictions were imposed on those living in these ghettos from children not being able to go to school to a ban on religious ceremonies and holidays. But often these carried on in secret to keep some semblance of a normal life. The ration of food that was allowed into these neighborhoods was meager, and many began to starve and suffer as a result.

At certain times and in different cities, Jews would be rounded up, taken out, forced to dig large graves, and then shot. These mass shootings were widespread and were the main choice of killing by the Einsatzgruppen, the group of men moving through Russia with the German army.

But the ghettos were not just to keep the Jews in one place, they were also created as temporary confines until they could be moved to their final destination: extermination camps.

CONCENTRATION CAMPS

Six camps had been built in Poland especially for the purpose of killing large groups of undesirables at a time, mainly Jews: Treblinka, Auschwitz-Birkenau, Belzec, Chelmno, Majdanek, and Sobibor (Berenbaum, 2018).

Children at Auschwitz

Prisoners were squashed into freight car trains to be transported on long journeys to the camps with hardly any water, food, or air. Many died along the way from starvation, dehydration, or suffocation. On arrival, a doctor would select those who were sick, very young, old, or pregnant to be processed first, and led directly to the gas chambers.

The rest were allocated colored triangles on their uniforms depending on their status; red meant political prisoners, purple was for Jehovah's Witnesses, green and black for criminals, homosexuals were given pink, while Jews had two yellow triangles overlapping to form the Star of David. At Auschwitz, all detainees were tattooed with a number to keep track of the prisoners.

Those who were seen as fit enough were forced to work, often dying from exhaustion, excessive beatings from the guards, malnutrition, or disease before they even reached the gas chambers. The average length of time in a camp that a prisoner stayed alive was just three months!

Most died in the gas chambers. This was known as the "Final Solution." Large groups were herded into a room where they were ordered to strip off all their clothes and possessions before entering what they were told were "showers." The doors were shut, and carbon monoxide pumped in, or Zyklon-B pellets tossed in. It took up to 20 minutes for all two thousand in the chamber to die, those closest to the gas vents first, while the rest screamed and clawed at the doors until they finally collapsed (Auschwitz-Birkenau, 2022).

Getting rid of the bodies caused another problem for the Nazis as there were so many. Groups of Jewish prisoners were tasked with removing everything from hair, tooth fillings, and jewelry to artificial limbs before the corpses were buried in deep pits. But after reassessing the situation, Himmler ordered huge crematoria to be built at the camps for quicker disposal, so the bodies could be burned (Berenbaum, 2018). They operated like factories, receiving people, killing them, and disposing of the remains as efficiently as possible with the least amount of cost. Between 4,000 and 8,000 were burned each day (Auschwitz-Birkenau, 2022).

In total, 6 million Jews were killed during the Nazi's reign, with over 3 million exterminated in these camps (Berenbaum, 2018). That was about a third of all the Jews in the world at that time.

Auschwitz Camp

ANNE FRANK

The history of the Holocaust would not be complete without the insight from the diaries of Anne Frank.

This book tells the story of a girl and her family that moved to the Netherlands when Hitler came into power. It details how they had to hide after the Germans invaded the Netherlands and began rounding up Jews. They were discovered after two years and sent off to Auschwitz where they were split up as a family, Anne and her mother eventually died from disease.

Otto Frank, her father, returned after the war, found the diary, and published it in 1947 (Tikkanen, 2017). It's one of the closest writings we have of the terror and horror that Jews faced during that time.

THE END AND AFTERMATH

When the Allies finally broke the Nazi army, and Hitler committed suicide, the Holocaust ended as well. But the pain and hardship did not end there.

Around 7 to 9 million people had been displaced or moved out of their original countries (Berenbaum, 2018). Most of these returned but others refused. Life could not be normal again going back to places where they had been hunted and tortured.

The pressure to create a homeland was one of the driving reasons that the State of Israel was established in May 1948, and refugees were allowed to move there (Berenbaum, 2018). But the issue of the concentration camps still posed a problem—the atrocities were so shocking, and in direct contravention of every humane law that justice had to be served to right the wrongs.

The Nuremberg Trials in 1945–1946 tried 22 Nazi officials for different war crimes, among them was the events at the camps (Berenbaum, 2018). Others like Einsatzgruppen members, commanders, and German generals were also charged, but many escaped or had already committed suicide.

Other trials took place as Nazi leaders were tracked down and found:

- In 1961, Adolf Eichmann who supervised the train transport to the camps was tried in Jerusalem.
- In 1987, Klaus Barbie was brought to justice for ordering Jews to be killed.
- In 1998, Maurice Papon had to answer for deporting 1,600 Jews.

What shocked the world the most was the extent of the genocide that took place, and how well-organized it all was. It was not a rampant hatred, but a systematic cleansing of Jews from the Third Reich.

17

HOW THE WAR CHANGED THE WORLD

The way the world had worked before was gone. The European colonial empires had become a thing of the past, giving way to massive superpowers. But the lesson of all-out war had been learned, and a different confrontation would now play out between these nations in the Cold War. There was a new set of politics ruling the world, and new inventions that were changing the way it all functioned.

GEO-POLITICAL

Many cities were left in ruins after the war. More than 70% of Germany's houses were gone as were 70,000 Soviet villages. Countries and their borders had shifted. Those nations that had been under German or Japanese rule had to be re-established. Orphans needed families. There was little food anywhere in Europe, and people starved. They had no homes, and the newly restored sovereign nation of Czechoslovakia pushed 3 million Germans from their borders, Poland did the same with over 1 million.

Refugees by the thousands looked for places to stay (MacMillan, 2017).

Normandy Gravesite

A massive shift in countries and their borders took place. Germany faced the biggest cuts as it was divided into two parts; Eastern and Western, with Berlin being quartered as a preventative measure to never have WW2 repeated. Japan was stripped of its army and overseen by the Allies. In 1947, Britain pulled out of India as a colonial power, leaving two new countries of Pakistan and India, Indonesia and much of Africa followed shortly after as they sought independence (MacMillan, 2017).

But it was Russia that gained the most in the upheaval. Most of the countries they had swarmed across to reach Hitler, they simply held onto, swallowing them into the new, expanded Soviet Union. This set up a new precedent between democracy in the west, and communism in the east, with the United States and USSR becoming superpowers.

The Nuremberg Trials were set up to try and hold those responsible for their actions in the war, and senior Nazis and Japanese generals like Hideki Tojo were put in the dock with some being executed and others imprisoned for life (MacMillan, 2017).

AMAZING FACTS

- *Hiroo Onoda, a Japanese officer, never surrendered after the war and held his position in the Philippines until he was formally relieved of duty in 1974 (Mighty, 2015).*

SOCIETY

Massive changes occurred within each country as cities swelled with many people moving from the countryside. Urbanization was on the increase. Women's roles were also on the rise as they had played pivotal parts in the war effort. With most of the men at war, it had been up to them to maintain farms, factories, and industry. As a result, women's rights began to be noticed, and in France and Italy, they were given the chance to vote for the first time (MacMillan, 2017).

One of the most significant outcomes of WW2 was the number of babies. During the war, the number of rapes that occurred by the Red Army as they moved through Europe is said to have ended in 2 million abortions every year from 1945 to 1948 (MacMillan, 2017). While many more newborns were the result of relationships that had happened between soldiers passing through countries as they fought and local women.

But in the United States, the opposite happened as families rebuilt. They were reunited and felt secure, and wanted a future together, leading to the Baby Boom. This was a period between 1946 and 1964 that saw an average of just over 4 million new babies every year (Khan Academy, 2008).

Racism had shown its ugly head in Germany with the Holocaust, and it was a reality that had to be dealt with, not just with Jews, but amongst those of color and different ethnic groups. In the United States, although the military was segregated during WW2, President Truman abolished those lines in the military. It took much longer for the whole country to scrap all segregation laws.

TECHNOLOGY

The need for superior weapons and supplies during the war had pushed both the Allies and the Axis Powers to invest heavily in research. The result was astounding and proved to be a massive leap forward in technology for the entire world.

The Nazis brought out cutting-edge equipment that could have won them the war if they had had more time to refine and produce these products. The V2 rocket and jet engines were among their top achievements.

Radar played a massive role in the Battle of the Atlantic, other sea skirmishes, and air confrontations, and would later be used to track civilian planes and storms (Little, 2021). The birth of the computer, one of the biggest breakthroughs of the 20th century, was a result of Alan Turing and other inventors' innovative ideas (Copeland, 2019).

But it was not just technology that profited, scientific advances were made in medicine. The first flu vaccine was used in the United States in 1945, and penicillin, which had been discovered in 1928, was widely produced for troops (Little, 2021). Even blood plasma transfusions, which made it easier to administer transfer of blood to patients during a battle, were formulated by Charles Drew for the military.

UNITED NATIONS AND WHO

The League of Nations had been such a joke that a new body needed to be formed where countries were committed, and there were repercussions for any actions that were seen as antagonistic. The birth of the United Nations initially saw The Big Three as its main contributors but made way for China to join in discussions. In the end, 51 nations signed and became members on October 24, 1945 (Lynch, 2018). Overall, the UN proved to be better organized and had much more say in worldwide events with its own security detail.

It also led to the formation of the World Health Organization (WHO) to cope with the aftermath of the war as well as disease and illnesses going forward.

THE COLD WAR

Probably the most significant outcome of WW2 was the emergence of a new conflict. On February 9, Premier Joseph Stalin gave a speech in which he declared that war between the East and West was inevitable. On March 5, 1946, Winston Churchill coined the term "Cold War," warning *"From Stettin in the Baltic to Trieste in the Adriatic, an iron curtain has descended across the continent,"* and called for a strengthening of Anglo-American ties as well as *"a new unity in Europe from which no nation should be permanently outcast"* (Encyclopedia Britannica, 1946).

With a full confrontation between the new superpowers out of the question because of the threat of nuclear weapons, other means of gaining the upper hand were followed leading to subversion, espionage, and backing wars in other smaller countries. The Cold War was an intense stand-off between the United States and USSR that came close to blowing up during the Cuban Missile Crisis.

But Stalin's agenda, with the rise of Communist China, made it impossible to ignore the threat, and the United States could no longer remain neutral. The Truman Doctrine in 1947 made it clear that the United States would fight against communism, and the Marshall Plan provided financial aid to post-war Europe to stabilize the economy and promote democracy (Khan Academy, 2008).

With the eastern parts of Europe amalgamated into an Eastern Bloc under the Soviets, and their break from the UN years later to form the Warsaw Pact, it was clear that there would be no agreement between western democracy and eastern communism. The Olympic Games and other sports arenas became a new battleground as each side *fought* for supremacy. The Cold War would last for another 45 years until communism in Russia collapsed.

CONCLUSION

An event of the magnitude of WW2 cannot easily be forgotten or ignored. The effects and memories are like scars that may heal on the outside, once cities are rebuilt and society carries on, but the damage and horror that people had to endure can never fully be washed away or covered so easily.

Many may have risen to the occasion inspiring acts of heroism, bravery, and courage, but it also brought out the worst in nations. Fascism, racism, and greed for power steered thousands of people to commit terrible acts of savagery against fellow humans, even genocide. There was suffering on both sides—the winners and the losers. The Allies may have been victorious, but at what cost?

History is there as a teacher to help us learn which mistakes we should never repeat. The threat of war, genocide, and racism has not disappeared because a treaty was signed. They are very real issues that can raise their heads again. If we are to learn from WW2, then it is to take note of what took place, the good and the bad.

We too can stand against those things that have ravaged the world. It all starts with tolerance and understanding, love and acceptance—for every color, creed, religion, ethnicity, and personality! War can never be the answer, even if it's one that's as small as in your own home!

"The greatest victory is that which requires no battle."
–Sun Tzu from the *Art of War*

If you have read this far, you have achieved the final goal! But it's not all about reaching the end, it's about the journey to get there, and what we learn along the way. If you enjoyed this ride through WW2 with me, there's always another journey.

Look out for more military history books, and sign up to my email list for more updates at james-burrows.com

REFERENCES

Admin. (2021, May 13). *Top 18 Joachim Peiper Quotes*. Inspirational Web. https://inspirationalweb.org/joachim-peiper-quotes/

The Allied Campaign in Italy, 1943–45: A Timeline, Part One. (2022b, May 23). The National WWII Museum. https://www.nationalww2museum.org/war/articles/allied-campaign-italy-1943-45-timeline-part-one

Andrews, E. (2015, July 10). *10 Surprising Facts About the Battle of Britain*. History. https://www.history.com/news/10-things-you-should-know-about-the-battle-of-britain

Andrews, E. (2016, September 8). *The Siege of Leningrad*. History. https://www.history.com/news/the-siege-of-leningrad

Andrews, E. (2018, August 31). *8 Things You May Not Know About the Battle of the Bulge*. History. https://www.history.com/news/8-things-you-may-not-know-about-the-battle-of-the-bulge

Arun. (2020, September 18). *10 Major Causes of World War II*. Learnodo Newtonic. https://learnodo-newtonic.com/world-war-2-causes

Atkins, H. (2018). *10 Facts About the Atomic Bombing of Hiroshima and Nagasaki*. History Hit. https://www.historyhit.com/facts-about-the-atomic-bombing-of-hiroshima-and-nagasaki/

Audie Murphy. (2019). Arlington National Cemetery. https://www.arlingtoncemetery.mil/Explore/Notable-Graves/Medal-of-Honor-Recipients/World-War-II-MoH-recipients/Audie-Murphy

Axis Alliance in World War II. (2022, April 22). USHMM Encyclopedia. https://encyclopedia.ushmm.org/content/en/article/axis-powers-in-world-war-ii

The Baby Boom. (2008). Khan Academy. https://www.khanacademy.org/humanities/us-history/postwarera/postwar-era/a/the-baby-boom

Bancroft, C. (2022). *20 Facts You Might Not Know About the Coventry Blitz*. Coventry City Council. https://www.coventry.gov.uk/coventry-blitz/20-facts-might-not-know-coventry-blitz

Battle of Britain | European History [1940]. (2019). Encyclopedia Britannica. https://www.britannica.com/event/Battle-of-Britain-European-history-1940

Battle of the Atlantic—WWII Timeline (September 3rd, 1939–May 7th, 1945). (2022). Second World War History. https://www.secondworldwarhistory.com/battle-of-the-atlantic.php

Battle of the Bulge. (2000). U.S. Army. https://www.army.mil/botb/

The Battle of Kursk: The Largest Tank Battle in History. (n.d.). Sky History TV Channel. https://www.history.co.uk/article/the-battle-of-kursk-the-largest-tank-battle-in-history

The Battle of Midway. (1999). The National WWII Museum. https://www.nationalww2museum.org/war/articles/battle-midway

The Battle of Monte Cassino. (n.d.-a). The Holocaust Explained. https://www.theholocaustexplained.org/life-in-nazi-occupied-europe/the-second-world-war/battle-of-monte-cassino/

Benito Mussolini. (2018, August 21). A&E Television Networks. https://www.history.com/topics/world-war-ii/benito-mussolini

Berenbaum, M. (2018). *Holocaust | Definition, Concentration Camps, & History*. Encyclopedia Britannica. https://www.britannica.com/event/Holocaust

Beyer, G. (2013). *Hermann Goering*. Jewish Virtual Library. https://www.jewishvirtuallibrary.org/hermann-goering

Beyer, G. (2022a, April 22). *Gallant & Heroic: The South African Contribution to World War II*. The Collector. https://www.thecollector.com/heroic-south-african-contributions-world-war-2/

Beyer, G. (2022b, June 8). *10 Things You May Not Know About the Battle of Stalingrad*. The Collector. https://www.thecollector.com/battle-of-stalingrad-facts/

Bhanbhagta Gurung. (n.d.). Traces of War. https://www.tracesofwar.com/persons/17/Bhanbhagta-Gurung.htm

Bibby, M. (n.d.). *Fighting Jack Churchill*. Historic UK. https://www.historic-uk.com/HistoryUK/HistoryofBritain/Fighting-Jack_Churchill/

Bluhm, R. K. (2022, September 10). *Operation Market Garden | Description & Facts*. Encyclopedia Britannica. https://www.britannica.com/event/Operation-Market-Garden

Boissoneault, L. (2017, July 19). *The True Story of Dunkirk as Told Through the Heroism of the "Medway Queen."* Smithsonian Magazine. https://www.smithsonianmag.com/history/true-story-dunkirk-told-through-heroism-medway-queen-180964105/

Bong—Maj Richard Ira Bong. (n.d.). Air Force Historical Support Division. https://www.afhistory.af.mil/FAQs/Fact-Sheets/Article/639628/bong-maj-richard-ira-bong/

Britain Alone. (2017, July). National Army Museum. https://www.nam.ac.uk/explore/britain-alone-1940

Browne, A. (2018). *The German Invasion of Poland in Numbers—1 September 1939*. History Hit. https://www.historyhit.com/the-german-invasion-of-poland-in-numbers-1-september-1939/

Brunies, R. (2021, July 14). *The Fascist King: Victor Emmanuel III of Italy*. The National WWII Museum. https://www.nationalww2museum.org/war/articles/fascist-king-victor-emmanuel-iii-italy

Campion, M. J. (2014, October 23). *How the World Loved the Swastika—Until Hitler Stole it.* BBC News. https://www.bbc.com/news/magazine-29644591

Carter, I. (2018, June 27). *Operation "Barbarossa" and Germany's Failure in the Soviet Union.* Imperial War Museums. https://www.iwm.org.uk/history/operation-barbarossa-and-germanys-failure-in-the-soviet-union

Chapple, A. (2019, November 23). *Winter War: The 1939 Soviet Invasion of Finland in Crystal-Clear Photos.* RadioFreeEurope/RadioLiberty. https://www.rferl.org/a/finlands-winter-war-with-the-soviet-union/30280490.html

Cooper, P. (2016, February 25). *A Single Bread Costs 4.6 Million During Germany's Hyperinflation in 1923.* History Daily. https://historydaily.org/germany-hyperinflation

Copeland, B. J. (2019). *Alan Turing | Biography, Facts, & Education.* Encyclopedia Britannica. https://www.britannica.com/biography/Alan-Turing

Correll, J. T. (2018, November 27). *The Fall of France.* Air & Space Forces Magazine. https://www.airandspaceforces.com/article/The-Fall-of-France/

Daniel, A. (2019, January 14). *30 Astonishing Facts About World War II That Will Change the Way You View It Forever.* Best Life Online. https://bestlifeonline.com/world-war-2-facts/

Egorov, B. (2020, May 2). *10 Little Known Facts About the Battle of Berlin.* Russia Beyond. https://www.rbth.com/history/332090-10-facts-about-berlin-battle

Eileen Nearne: The Spy Who Foiled a Nazi Attack | About the Hero. (2019, September 11). Lowell Milken Center. https://www.lowellmilkencenter.org/programs/projects/view/eileen-nearne/hero

The Evacuation of Children During the Second World War. (2019). The History Press. https://www.thehistorypress.co.uk/articles/the-evacuation-of-children-during-the-second-world-war/

Facts About Pearl Harbor. (2018, October 27). Pearl Harbor Tours Blog. https://www.pearlharbortours.com/blog/facts-about-pearl-harbor

Fausone, J. (2018). *Virginia Hall*. Home of Heroes. https://homeofheroes.com/heroes-stories/world-war-ii/virginia-hall/

15 Things You Might Not Know About Pearl Harbor. (2016). AOP. https://www.aop.com/blog/15-things-you-might-not-know-about-pearl-harbor

5 Stories of Real-Life Escape Attempts by Allied Prisoners of War. (2022a). Imperial War Museums. https://www.iwm.org.uk/history/5-stories-of-real-life-escape-attempts-by-allied-prisoners-of-war

Franklin, S. (2017, July 28). *The Untold Story of Britain's POW Camps*. The Irish Times. https://www.irishtimes.com/culture/books/the-untold-story-of-britain-s-pow-camps-1.3169823

Garcia, J. M. (2009, September 16). *German POWs on the American Homefront*. Smithsonian Magazine. https://www.smithsonianmag.com/history/german-pows-on-the-american-homefront-141009996/

Gas Chambers—Auschwitz and Shoah. (2022). Auschwitz-Birkenau. https://www.auschwitz.org/en/history/auschwitz-and-shoah/gas-chambers/

The Guadalcanal Campaign | History of Western Civilization II. (2019). Lumen Learning. https://courses.lumenlearning.com/suny-hccc-worldhistory2/chapter/the-guadalcanal-campaign/

General George C. Marshall. (2019). PBS; WGBH. https://www.pbs.org/wgbh/americanexperience/features/macarthur-general-george-c-marshall/

German POW Camps in World War Two - History. (2018, July 6). History on the Net. https://www.historyonthenet.com/world-war-two-german-pow-camps

Gestapo | Nazi Political Police. (2018b). Encyclopedia Britannica. https://www.britannica.com/topic/Gestapo

Gilbert, A. (2018a). *The Blitz | World War II*. Encyclopedia Britannica. https://www.britannica.com/event/the-Blitz

Gilbert, A. (2018b). *Battles of El-Alamein | World War II*. Encyclopedia Britannica. https://www.britannica.com/event/battles-of-El-Alamein

Hansard 1803–2005. (2018). UK Parliament. https://api.parliament.uk/historic-hansard/index.html

Hays, J. (2016, November). *Brutal Treatment of POWs by the Japanese and Atrocities by U.S. Soldiers*. Facts and Details. https://factsanddetails.com/asian/ca67/sub427/item2531.html

Hershel Woodrow "Woody" Williams | World War II | U.S. Marine Corps Reserve | Medal of Honor Recipient. (2022). Congressional Medal of Honor Society. https://www.cmohs.org/recipients/hershel-woodrow-woody-williams

Hewitt, N. (n.d.). *Operation Torch | Allied Military Strategy*. Encyclopedia Britannica. https://www.britannica.com/topic/Operation-Torch

Hitler, A. (1999). *Mein Kampf*. Houghton Mifflin. https://www.sjsu.edu/people/mary.pickering/courses/His146/s1/MeinKampfpartone0001.pdf

Hogeback, J. (2019). *How the Symbolism of the Swastika was Ruined*. Encyclopedia Britannica. https://www.britannica.com/story/how-the-symbolism-of-the-swastika-was-ruined

How Did Adolf Hitler Happen? (2022a). The National WWII Museum. https://www.nationalww2museum.org/war/articles/how-did-adolf-hitler-happen

How Neutral Norway Fell to the German Blitzkrieg in 1940. (2018). Imperial War Museums. https://www.iwm.org.uk/history/how-neutral-norway-fell-to-the-german-blitzkrieg-in-1940

Hudson, M. (2018). *Battle of Iwo Jima | World War II*. Encyclopedia Britannica. https://www.britannica.com/topic/Battle-of-Iwo-Jima

Huxen, K. (2017, July 12). *Operation Husky: The Allied Invasion of Sicily*. The National WWII Museum. https://www.nationalww2museum.org/war/articles/operation-husky-allied-invasion-sicily

The Invasion of the Soviet Union and the Beginnings of Mass Murder. (2019). Yadvashem. https://www.yadvashem.org/holocaust/about/final-solution-beginning/mass-murder-in-ussr.html

Japanese Relocation During World War II. (2017, April 10). National Archives. https://www.archives.gov/education/lessons/japanese-relocation

Keegan, J. (2018). *Normandy Invasion | Definition, Map, Photos, Casualties, & Facts.* Encyclopedia Britannica. https://www.britannica.com/event/Normandy-Invasion

Kelly, E. (2017, September 21). *The True Story of Desmond Doss was Too Heroic Even for "Hacksaw Ridge."* All That's Interesting. https://allthatsinteresting.com/desmond-doss

Kimball, D. G. (n.d.). *Reality Check: The Atomic Bombings of Hiroshima & Nagasaki.* Arms Control Association. https://www.armscontrol.org/pressroom/2020-07/reality-check-atomic-bombings-hiroshima-nagasaki

Kinder, John M. (2014). *A War of Many Names.* Oklahoma Humanities, 8.

Klein, C. (2016, November 7). *The Daring Escape That Forged Winston Churchill.* History. https://www.history.com/news/the-daring-escape-that-forged-winston-churchill

Knighton, A. (2017, May 25). *A Terrible Mistake—Why the USSR Ignored Britain's Warnings of Impending Invasion.* War History Online. https://www.warhistoryonline.com/world-war-ii/russia-ignored-british-warnings-german-invasion-xb.html?chrome=1

Levin-Areddy, A. J. (2018, November 1). *13 Facts About Benito Mussolini.* Mental Floss. https://www.mentalfloss.com/article/560588/facts-about-benito-mussolini

Little, B. (2021, April 26). *6 World War II Innovations That Changed Everyday Life.* History. https://www.history.com/news/world-war-ii-innovations

Lynch, C. M. (2018). *United Nations | History, Organization, Functions, & Facts*. Encyclopedia Britannica. https://www.britannica.com/topic/United-Nations

MacMillan, M. (2017, September 7). *Rebuilding the World After the Second World War*. The Guardian. https://www.theguardian.com/world/2009/sep/11/second-world-war-rebuilding

The Main Commanders and Best Generals of WWII. (n.d.). D-Day Eyewitness Accounts of WWII. https://www.normandy1944.info/home/commanders

Manaev, G. (2021, November 3). *How German Prisoners of War Lived and Died in the USSR*. Russia Beyond. https://www.rbth.com/history/334372-german-prisoners-of-war-in-ussr

Mansoor, P. R. (2019, June 24). *Operation Bagration and the Destruction of the Army Group Center*. Hoover Institution. https://www.hoover.org/research/operation-bagration-and-destruction-army-group-center

Merridale, C. (2011, July 28). *Stalin's Order No. 227: "Not a Step Back."* The History Reader. https://www.thehistoryreader.com/military-history/stalins-order-227-step-back

Mighty, T. (2015, August 8). *21 Rare and Weird Facts About World War II*. Insider. https://www.insider.com/21-rare-and-weird-facts-about-world-war-2-2015-8

Monte Cassino Monastery: Miraculously Rebuilt After WWII Bombing. (2018, January 22). Grand Voyage Italy. http://www.grandvoyageitaly.com/travel/monte-cassino-monastery-miraculously-rebuilt-after-wwii-bombing

National-Socialist German Workers' Party. (2019). Encyclopedia. https://www.encyclopedia.com/politics/legal-and-political-magazines/national-socialist-german-workers-party

Nazi Party | Definition, Meaning, History, & Facts. (2018a). Encyclopedia Britannica. https://www.britannica.com/topic/Nazi-Party

Neikirk, T. (2022, February 8). *6 Things We Didn't Know About the Guadalcanal Campaign*. War History Online. https://www.warhistoryonline.com/world-war-ii/guadalcanal-campaign-facts.html

Nielsen, D. (2019, November 11). *World War II Facts, Turning Points, Battles, and More*. FamilySearch Blog. https://www.familysearch.org/en/blog/world-war-2-facts

Noy, U. (2019). *World War 2 Leaders*. 2worldwar2.com. https://www.2worldwar2.com/leaders.htm

Obituary: Jane Fawcett. (2016, May 26). The Sydney Morning Herald. https://www.smh.com.au/national/obituary-jane-fawcett-20160526-gp4a7g.htm

Orlikoff, A. J. (n.d.). *Douglas MacArthur—Biographies*. National Museum of the United States Army. https://www.thenmusa.org/biographies/douglas-macarthur/

Parkin, S. (2018, August 13). *5 Major Causes of World War Two in Europe*. History Hit. https://www.historyhit.com/causes-of-world-war-two-in-europe/

Pelzer, K. (2020, August 22). *How to Use Wisdom to "Know Your Enemy"—Here are the 75 Best Sun Tzu Quotes*. Parade. https://parade.com/1074916/kelseypelzer/sun-tzu-quotes/

Pitogo, H. (2013, September 30). *24 Real Heroes of World War II (Part 1)*. War History Online. https://www.warhistoryonline.com/articles/25-heroes-world-war-ii.html

POWs in the USA—10 Surprising Facts About America's WWII Prisoner of War Camps. (2018, April 11). Military History Now. https://militaryhistorynow.com/2018/04/10/pows-in-the-usa-10-amazing-facts-about-americas-ww2-prisoner-of-war-camps/

Ray, M. (2020a). *Battle of Okinawa—Intensification and Collapse of Japanese Resistance*. Encyclopedia Britannica. https://www.britannica.com/topic/Battle-of-Okinawa/Intensification-and-collapse-of-Japanese-resistance

Ray, M. (2020b). *The Attack on Pearl Harbor*. Encyclopedia Britannica. https://www.britannica.com/story/the-attack-on-pearl-harbor

Redhead. (2018). *10 Facts About the Battle of Kursk*. History Hit. https://www.historyhit.com/facts-about-the-battle-of-kursk/

Ringer Edwards: Australian WWII POW Who Survived Being Crucified for 63 Hours. (2022, June 26). SOFREP Media Group. https://sofrep.com/news/ringer-edwards-australian-wwii-pow-who-survived-being-crucified-for-63-hours/

Robinson, M. (2020, April 14). *The Battle of Berlin 1945—A Day-by-Day Account*. Berlin Experiences. https://www.berlinexperiences.com/the-battle-of-berlin-1945-a-day-by-day-account/

Roos, D. (2019, March 12). *D-Day: Facts on the Epic 1944 Invasion That Changed the Course of WWII*. History. https://www.history.com/news/d-day-normandy-wwii-facts

Royde-Smith, J. G. (2018). *Operation Barbarossa | European History*. Encyclopedia Britannica. https://www.britannica.com/event/Operation-Barbarossa

Russo-Finnish War | Summary, Combatants, & Facts. (2018c). Encyclopedia Britannica. https://www.britannica.com/event/Russo-Finnish-War

The Second World War. (2019). Returned & Services League of Australia. https://www.rslnsw.org.au/commemoration/australias-military-heritage/the-second-world-war/

Sedgwick, E. (2019, November 7). *10 Heartbreaking Facts About the Warsaw Ghetto*. Listverse. https://listverse.com/2019/11/07/warsaw-ghetto-facts/

Simha, R. K. (2016, July 18). *How India Bailed Out the West in World War II*. Indian Defence Review. http://www.indiandefencereview.com/spotlights/how-india-bailed-out-the-west-in-world-war-ii/

6 Things You May Not Know About POWs in England During the First World War. (2018, October 23). The Historic England Blog. https://heritagecalling.com/2018/10/23/6-things-you-may-not-know-about-pows-in-england-during-the-first-world-war/

Sterner, D. (2022). *Matt Urban—Recipient*. Military Times Valor. https://valor.militarytimes.com/hero/2325

Tedeschi, D. (2020, October). *Erich Hartmann, the Most Successful Fighter Pilot of All Time*. Smithsonian Magazine. https://www.smithsonianmag.com/air-space-magazine/who-was-erich-hartmann-180975845/

Ten Things You May Not Know About the Battle of El Alamein (1942). (2016, July 7). History Collection. https://historycollection.com/ten-things-may-not-know-anout-battle-el-alamein-1942/

Thatcher, J. (2008). *Winston S Churchill: We Shall Fight on the Beaches*. YouTube. https://www.youtube.com/watch?v=MkTw3_PmKtc

Tikkanen, A. (2017). *Diary of a Young Girl | Anne Frank, History & Facts*. Encyclopedia Britannica. https://www.britannica.com/topic/The-Diary-of-a-Young-Girl

Tovy, T. (2015). *From the Nisshin to the Musashi: The Military Career of Admiral Yamamoto Isoroku*. Association for Asian Studies. https://www.asianstudies.org/publications/eaa/archives/from-the-nisshin-to-the-musashi-the-military-career-of-admiral-yamamoto-isoroku/

Treaties, States Parties, and Commentaries—Geneva Convention on Prisoners of War, 1929. (n.d.). International Committee of the Red Cross. https://ihl-databases.icrc.org/applic/ihl/ihl.nsf/52d68d14de6160e0c12563da005fdb1b/eb1571b00daec90ec125641e00402aa6

The Treatment of Soviet POWs: Starvation, Disease, and Shootings, June 1941–January 1942. (2019). USHMM Encyclopedia. https://encyclopedia.ushmm.org/content/en/article/the-treatment-of-soviet-pows-starvation-disease-and-shoot ings-june-1941january-1942

Tretheway, M. G. (1992, June 2). *Opinion | 1,046 Bombers but Cologne Lived*. The New York Times. https://www.nytimes.com/1992/06/02/opinion/IHT-1046-bombers-but-cologne-lived.html

Trouillard, S. (2022, August 23). *"They Would Have Preferred Hell": The Battle of Stalingrad, 80 Years On*. France 24. https://www.france24.com/en/europe/20220823-they-would-have-preferred-hell-the-battle-of-stalingrad-80-years-on

25 Interesting Facts About Prisoners of War. (2015, July 13). Kickass Facts. https://www.kickassfacts.com/25-interesting-facts-about-prisoners-of-war/

Vasily Chuikov. (2022). Liberation Route Europe. https://www.liberationroute.com/stories/212/vasily-chuikov

The Warsaw Ghetto Uprising. (n.d.-b). The Holocaust Explained. https://www.theholocaustexplained.org/the-camps/the-warsaw-ghetto-a-case-study/the-warsaw-uprising/

What You Need to Know About the Battle of the River Plate. (2022b). Imperial War Museums. https://www.iwm.org.uk/history/what-you-need-to-know-about-the-battle-of-the-river-plate

When Nazis Tried to Trace Aryan Race Myth in Tibet. (2021, September 14). BBC News. https://www.bbc.com/news/world-asia-india-58466528

Why Colonel Ruby Bradley was Known as the Angel in Fatigues—Medals. (2022). Identify Medals. https://www.identifymedals.com/article/why-colonel-ruby-bradley-was-known-as-the-angel-in-fatigues/

Winston Churchill Gives His Famous Speech "The Few" in the House of Commons. (2022, October 5). British Heritage. https://britishheritage.com/history/winston-churchill-famous-speech-few

World War II. (2009, October 29). A&E Television Networks. https://www.history.com/topics/world-war-ii/world-war-ii-history

World War II: Timeline. (2018). USHMM Encyclopedia. https://encyclopedia.ushmm.org/content/en/article/world-war-ii-key-dates

Wueschner, Dr. S. (2019, February 11). *Operation Argument ("Big Week"): The Beginning of the End of the German Luftwaffe*. Maxwell Air Force Base. https://www.maxwell.af.mil/News/Display/Article/1754049/operation-argument-big-week-the-beginning-of-the-end-of-the-german-luftwaffe/

IMAGE REFERENCES

12019. (2013, January 30). *Allied Generals*. [Image]. Pixabay. https://pixabay.com/photos/world-war-ii-allies-generals-76645/

Dimitrisvetsikas1969. (2020, January 30). *Children at Auschwitz*. [Image]. Pixabay. https://pixabay.com/photos/auschwitz-concentration-camp-4803494/

Janeb13. (2016, February 1). *Okinawa*. [Image]. Pixabay. https://pixabay.com/photos/war-soldiers-marines-okinawa-battle-1172111/

Library Of Congress. (2020, January 27). *President Roosevelt*. [Image]. Unsplash. https://unsplash.com/photos/6aDvguLNOik

Marjan Blan. (2019, September 10). *[UKRAINE. Kiev. 2019. Kiev Children's Railway. Museum] (Josef Stalin)*. [Image]. Unsplash. https://unsplash.com/photos/dRmmRiuniig

Marsjo. (2019, February 11). *Normandy Gravesite*. [Image]. Pixabay. https://pixabay.com/photos/omaha-beach-normandy-france-d-day-3987540/

Museumsvictoria. (2019, October 23). *77 Squadron RAF*. [Image]. Unsplash. https://unsplash.com/photos/oyGmigXV030

Peter89ba. (2018, September 14). *Auschwitz Camp*. [Image]. Pixabay. https://pixabay.com/photos/auschwitz-i-enlightenment-poland-3671388/

Simon_Goodall. (2022, January 11) *Winston Churchill*. [Image]. Pixabay. https://pixabay.com/photos/churchill-winston-britain-scotland-6924619/

Southtree. (2016, March 29). *Germans Changing Signs*. [Image]. Pixabay. https://pixabay.com/photos/world-war-ii-automatic-truck-car-1287778/

Tislas. (2018, November 17). *Iwo Jima Statue*. [Image]. Pixabay. https://pixabay.com/photos/iwo-jima-military-flag-monument-3820507/

WikiImages. (2012, December 12) *Cologne Bombing*. [Image] Pixabay. https://pixabay.com/photos/cologne-bombing-destruction-war-63176/

WikiImages. (2012, December 5). *Carrier Capsize*. [Image]. Pixabay. https://pixabay.com/photos/fluzeugtraeger-capsize-bombing-62822/

WikiImages. (2012, December 5). *Field Marshal Montgomery*. [Image]. Pixabay. https://pixabay.com/photos/war-world-war-bernard-l-montgomery-62848/

WikiImages. (2012, November 28). *Pearl Harbor*. [Image]. Pixabay. https://pixabay.com/photos/pearl-harbor-ship-warship-destroyed-67756/

WikiImages. (2012, October 10). *Beach Landing*. [Image]. Pixabay. https://pixabay.com/photos/landing-landing-craft-normandy-60527/

WikiImages. (2013, January 3). *Atomic Bomb*. [Image]. Pixabay. https://pixabay.com/photos/mushroom-cloud-atomic-bomb-67534/

WikiImages. (2013, January 3). *Normandy Supply*. [Image]. Pixabay. https://pixabay.com/photos/normandy-supply-second-world-war-67545/

WikiImages. (2013, January 4). *Warsaw Ghetto*. [Image]. Pixabay. https://pixabay.com/photos/ghetto-warsaw-fear-child-armed-67736/

WikiImages. (2015, July 9). *Germany Surrenders Headline*. [Image]. Pixabay. https://pixabay.com/photos/the-stars-and-stripes-extra-newspaper-836027/

ABOUT THE AUTHOR

James is an armchair military expert, developing an early interest in military history from stories told by his Grandfathers and even his Great-Grandfather, who fought at the Somme.

Whether writing about WW2 or the American Revolutionary War, James hopes to spark a healthy curiosity and love for history in today's young people.

When not working or spending time with his wife and children, James can be found walking his two beautiful black labradors in the local countryside, pondering ideas for his next book.

Printed in Great Britain
by Amazon

50833413R00101